"Dr. Vicki Rackner gets it. She listens and has a true understanding of the day-to-day challenges hard-working, overwhelmed caregivers face. Then with compassion and humor she offers practical ideas about what steps to take next. On dark days, Dr. Vicki offers the light of hope and optimism. She helps people connect with caregiving as an act of love."

~Nancy Lewin, Director, The Caregiver Initiative
Johnson & Johnson Consumer Products Company

"Vicki Rackner, MD, offers the ultimate caregiver prescription—the knowledge that you are not alone, a roadmap for getting and staying connected, and the magical elixir of hope."

~Ed Hallowell, MD
Child and adult psychiatrist and best-selling author

"What a find. An easy-to-read, common-sense book about helping people be better caregivers by taking better care of themselves. Having been in the position of caregiver to both a child with a chronic illness and an ailing elderly parent, I wish I'd had a book like this to help guide my way. This should be required reading for everyone who steps up to the caregiving role."

~Linda J. Popky
President, L2M Associates, Inc.

D0905495

"Dr. Vicki Rackner is one of the few physicians who actively promotes the patient being involved in their own course of care. She understands the value of the patient taking a proactive role in directing and overseeing their medical care rather than just being vulnerable to what we now know as a very potentially dangerous (even fatal) journey to improved health. Dr. Rackner presents in a very pragmatic and understandable way useful tools for patients to better navigate our complex medical system. She also educates providers as to the importance of the patient-doctor relationship and how the transparency of information is crucial to the proper care of the patient."

~Louis Rubino, PhD, FACHE
Professor / Program Director
Health Administration Program
California State University

"Dr. Vicki Rackner was extremely helpful when our son was facing surgery. Dr. Vicki helped us in three ways: 1. by explaining the pros and cons of an operation vs letting nature take its course, 2. offering practical steps our son could take for the best outcome, and 3. setting expectations for recovery. Her easy-to-understand information enabled me to be more peaceful and confident about our choice to proceed."

~Cathy T.

"Dear Dr. Rackner...

"Thank you for your excellent, thoughtful advice concerning my wife's upcoming appointment with the neurosurgeon and second opinion. Metastatic breast cancer is scary enough, but throwing a brain tumor into the mix reduced me to a near babbling idiot. Your calm and forthright approach helped me to think it through and enabled us to successfully navigate those choppy seas. *You are truly the Suze Orman of medical advice!*"

~Dave P.

"Dr. Rackner is one of a kind! Her first and foremost interest is that of her patients, and she creates an environment of trust, truth, and acceptance. As an RN I knew immediately the level of professionalism, authenticity, and benevolence we were being exposed to was something Dr. Rackner's audiences get every time!"

~Sally Algiere

"This down-to-earth book firmly but gently reminds those caring for others that we cannot be effective unless we live fully in our own right. Far from advocating a me-first attitude, the book's author, herself an accomplished surgeon, speaks out of her own personal and professional experience. Her words will enlighten and endear you to her. Most important, her thoughts will transform you."

~Rabbi Edgar Weinsberg, EdD, DD
Patient health care educator and author,
Conquer Prostate Concer: How Medicine, Faith, Love and Sex Can Renew Your Life

"This is a definitive yet practical resource and an invaluable tool for Baby Boomers who are, or will soon become, caregivers. Through her wisdom, wit, and warmth, Dr. Rackner provides a roadmap to help caregivers navigate an often perilous and unplanned journey. She lets us peer through the lens of realism to assess ourselves, avoid pitfalls, and assists us to reach our destination without regrets. Peruse it ... read it ... USE it!"

~William Gillis
CEO, Parent Care, Inc.

"The best organized and most informative book I've seen on the subject—full of practical, instantly doable suggestions and ideas that strike at the heart of the issues we caregivers face every day. There's an 'aha' on every page!"

~David Balch
Speaker, author, *Cancer for Two*
Founder of The Patient/Partner Project and *CopingUniversity.com*

"In my profession as a coordinator for our local Area Agency on Aging, I have worked with family caregivers since 1997 and have had heartfelt connections with caregivers in all kinds of circumstances. I resonated with the unspoken pain, exhaustion, fear, and helplessness. Each felt hauntingly familiar to my own heartache [as a family caregiver]. This book is an easy read and contains timeless wisdom. I would recommend it to anyone looking for strength and support in their caregiving challenges."

~Jane Clear
Local Coordinator, Family Caregiver Support Program,
Aging and Long-Term Care, Washington State

CAREGIVING WITHOUT REGRETS

3 Steps to Avoid Burnout and Manage Disappointment, Guilt, and Anger

CAREGIVING WITHOUT REGRETS

3 Steps to Avoid Burnout and
Manage Disappointment, Guilt, and Anger

VICKI RACKNER, MD

President, Medical Bridges
Founder, The Caregiver Club

Medical Bridges
Seattle, Washington

Disclaimer: I'm not your doctor (and, if you're a smart patient or caregiver, neither are you). I care about you too much to be your doctor or even offer medical advice. You want the opinion of a doctor who knows your whole story and performs a complete evaluation. I hope to direct you to the right questions. Then you and your doctor can arrive at the answers that work best for you. Smart patients and empowered patient advocates turn to their doctors—and not to their neighbors or friends or favorite Web sites—for their diagnoses and treatment plans.

The author and publisher shall have neither liability nor responsibility to any person or entity with respect to any loss or damage caused, or alleged to have been caused, directly or indirectly by the information contained in this book.

Library of Congress Control Number: 2009927943

ISBN13: 978-0-9769430-3-7
ISBN10: 0-9769430-3-4

www.TheCaregiverClub.com
www.MedicalBridges.com
Published by Medical Bridges
    8441 SE 68th, Suite 298
    Mercer Island, WA 98040
    Phone: (425) 451-3777
    Email: DrRackner@MedicalBridges.com

Book Design, Production,
    Distribution and Marketing: Concierge Marketing, Inc., Omaha
Cover photo by Marianne McCoy

Printed in the United States
10   9   8   7   6   5   4   3   2   1

TO AUNT MOO MOO

When I was young, I wanted to change the world
but the world did not change.

Then I tried to change my town,
but the town did not change.

Then I tried to change my family,
but my family did not change.

Then, I knew—first, I must change myself.

~Rabbi Israel Salanter

CONTENTS

INTRODUCTION

I sat at my dying aunt's bedside, grateful that I didn't have any regrets. My care was given and received as an act of love. Our family did it our own eccentric way that worked for us.

My close relationship with my aunt had deepened under improbable circumstances. My aunt had flown into town to meet my newborn son just weeks after the death of her only daughter. On a sunny Monday morning walk, as we paused watching the ducks on the pond, it dawned on us. She just lost a daughter, and I just gained the need for motherly wisdom. We intentionally forged a new partnership cemented through our just-like-clockwork Sunday morning phone conversations.

Two years later, I got "the call." My aunt had cancer. Advanced cancer. I had read *Tuesdays with Morrie,* but I was now living Sundays with Aunt Moo Moo.

We joked that my aunt must have nine lives. For years she had defied all the medical odds as she survived cancer and then multiple life-threatening medical crises. My aunt had a habit of keeping her hospitalizations a secret as long as possible. I reminded her that I might be a useful person to have at her side. After all, I pointed out, I'm a surgeon who coaches patients to speak up.

She said, "No thanks, Honey. I hate having people with me at the hospital. It makes me feel like I'm dying. I'm not."

Eight years after the doctor declared my aunt had three to six months to live, my sort-of-mother used the last of her nine lives. Aunt Moo Moo was not a woo-woo person, so she surprised us when she told us about a dream in which her daughter delivered the message, "It's time." My aunt let the family gather at her bedside. We laughed and cried and silently held hands. We said a bittersweet goodbye to a most extraordinary woman.

My aunt and I shared years of caregiving at its absolute best. Was this an example of "practice makes perfect?" After all, my aunt and I were connected in caregiving for almost a dozen consecutive years, changing roles as if we were engaged in musical caregiver chairs. I supported my aunt as she cared for her daughter and then during her long illness when her husband was her primary caregiver. In between, my aunt supported me for the two years I worked through my son's medical problems, now gratefully resolved.

I learned the most through mistakes I made as I advocated for my son's health. I experienced caregiving at its absolute worst during this dark chapter of my life. I began with the best of intentions. In the darkness, though, I lost my way and took some wrong turns. I found myself on a slippery slope to caregiver burnout.

My son's diagnosis took all of us by surprise. When my aunt held my beautiful newborn son, she repeated the pediatrician's words: "He's perfect." Months into my son's life, subtle clues gave way to bigger clues that finally led to his diagnosis. I reorganized my life around a single-minded purpose: assuring my son would live his best life possible. Everything else, including my surgical career, friends, and even my marriage, took a back seat. I squeezed them in if and when I could.

I made virtually every caregiver mistake in the book. I treated myself as if I were the Energizer Bunny, pushing through the exhaustion known so well by both the parents of infants and caregivers of loved ones of every age. I took pride in the fact that my bladder could go ten or twelve hours between pit stops. I ate on the go and slept only enough to go on. My idea of exercise was taking the laundry up and down the stairs. Fun and joy were luxuries I thought I could not afford with my limited time and attention budget.

I engaged in indulgent thoughts and feelings that didn't lead to better mothering or better caregiving. I went to sleep most nights thinking that I was falling short. I felt guilty about the things I should not have done during my pregnancy that may have contributed to my son's situation. I managed the uncertainty about my son's future with worst-case scenarios that kept me up when I so needed sleep. I felt angry and betrayed. Why weren't things working out the way I imagined in my dreams?

When well-intentioned people offered advice about self-care, I just smiled politely, nodded my head, and dismissed them as clueless. Go for a ten-minute walk? If they only knew what it was like to walk in my shoes, I thought, they would understand how ridiculous it sounded. Those shoes already have too much walking to do.

As the months wore on, I found myself more fatigued, more isolated, and more overwhelmed. Some days a trip to the grocery store and the preparation of even a simple dinner were conquests well beyond my capacity. Even the search for the pizza delivery phone number seemed like a big job.

I got to the end of what I had to give before the need for my giving ended. Sometimes I wondered if I could go on for one more day or one more hour or even one more minute.

Fatigue from deep in my bones made me long for a nap or, better yet, a vacation from my life.

BECOME THE CAREGIVER YOU WANT TO BE

My son's medical issues completely resolved after about two years, but there was no big celebration. By that time I had lost my marriage, lost my career as I knew it, and lost my dreams. I lost myself. I could not go on living as I had. It was that simple. I knew I had to make radical changes, but how?

I started by taking an honest look at the consequences of my attempt to be the strong person who could do it alone. I put myself in the shoes of people who loved me. What was it like for them to stand by and watch me suffer when they knew they could help? It must have been like sitting at the kitchen table watching me starve because of my stubborn unwillingness to reach out for the abundance of food right there in front of me. My choices hurt the people I loved.

What about my son? I wanted him to be surrounded by joy and laughter and love. There was not a lot of that in our home.

Somehow, I started playing with the possibility that taking care of myself was an idea worth considering. I didn't do it for me; I did it for the benefit of the people I cared about. I wanted my son to have a happy mother who followed her passions. I wanted my friends and relatives to know the joy I got when I helped others in their time of need. I needed to learn how to accept help. I needed to take care of myself. Maybe that ten-minute walk I had dismissed wasn't so silly after all.

Slowly, I took one step after another that helped move toward the person, mother, and caregiver I wanted to be.

This book contains my hard-won lessons.

How do I describe my changes so that you can see if they will work for you too? Maybe a story from my son's toddler years can help. One day my three-year-old wanted to take a closer look at the big yellow trucks on a construction site. I pointed to the sturdy fence around the construction site and the sign on the closed gate.

"Do you see that sign?" I asked. "It says, 'Do not enter.'"

My son thought for a minute, then suggested, "Take down sign."

I took down the signs that announce the rules dedicated caregivers should follow. And I will show how you can do that too.

We build lives that matter just like construction workers build homes. **Caregiving, which can be a defining part of your personal legacy, is one of the most complex, challenging, and rewarding projects you will ever design and execute.** It works best when it's built on the solid foundation of your strengths and when you apply your best tools that bring success in other parts of your life.

WELCOME TO
THE CAREGIVERS' CLUB

Caregivers are like construction workers who leave their own projects to lend a helping hand on a buddy's site. At the height of a career, just after the birth of a baby, or maybe right before you retire, the need arises, and you've been drafted into the caregivers' club.

As I responded to my son's illness, I thought dedicated caregivers simply abandoned their own construction sites. They shut their own wants and needs behind closed gates festooned with signs that announce, "Do not enter." A good caregiver should be at the bedside of a hospitalized loved one 24/7, I thought. A good caregiver should not experience guilt or anger or take time to exercise or abandon a loved one in pain to indulge in frivolity with friends.

When you try to lock away your own wants and needs, someone pays. Usually everyone pays. You're not fun to be around. Your work, relationships, and even caregiving suffer. The person for whom you care feels it, and they can begin to feel like a burden on you.

Believe it or not, you are best able to serve others as the person you are rather than the person someone else wants you to be or needs you to be. You can throw out the caregiving rule book and mold your caregiving to your unique circumstances.

When it was time for my son to get a retainer, his orthodontist did not take ten retainers off the shelf and try each to see what worked best. There might be an occasional perfect fit, but most of his patients would wind up with an impaired ability to speak clearly and enjoy food. Instead, the orthodontist took an impression of my son's teeth and made a custom retainer. Custom caregiving that fits you works best. That's what this book is about.

Your life circumstances are one of a kind. You may be caring for a parent or a child or a partner. You may be working as a health care professional, volunteering in your community, or reaching out to victims of poverty or natural disasters or disease. You may care for a loved one who lives with you, a neighbor next door, or someone you never met from across the globe. You may help an otherwise healthy person recover from an accident, assist someone with a chronic illness, or offer comfort and companionship to someone with an incurable disease. The final goodbye may be years or months or days away.

Even though each caregiver has a different story, most caregivers share a core struggle. How can you reach out to alleviate the suffering of others and continue to give with an open heart? How do you avoid the immobilizing despair family caregivers call burnout and community relief workers call compassion fatigue? Here are my hard-won caregiving lessons in three simple steps:

- Be who you are.
- Know what you know.
- Do what you need to do.

I know how tired and busy you are, and I wish I could end there. You could use a nap right about now. I don't want to add one more thing to your to-do list. I promise that every moment you invest either reading a page or trying something new will be rewarded with more time or more energy or more resources that will ease your caregiver burden.

KNOW WHEN GOOD ENOUGH IS GOOD ENOUGH

My goal in writing this book is to help you do the following:

- Understand the inherent challenges of caregiving
- Gather greater insight about yourself
- Trust that good enough is good enough
- Share the caregiving with others
- Learn how you can care for yourself and know why you must
- Keep hope alive
- Evolve into the best caregiver you can be

My aunt was the kind of person who would be pleased to think that her hardships made your life easier. I hope that you experience caregiving as the act of love it is and flourish in the process, just like my aunt and I did. I hope that the changes I made can help you be your best and give your best.

One day you will cross the caregiver finish line. Sometimes it's a happy ending. The oncologist tells you good news after the final round of chemotherapy. The neurologist notes the full recovery of function after a stroke. The family you sponsor is in a rebuilt home after the earthquake. Most caregivers open their hearts to people winding down to the final goodbye. My fondest wish for you is that when you finally get to the finish line you look back with no regrets.

1

BE WHO YOU ARE

Jan intuitively knew the lessons I had learned through my misadventures in caregiving. When Jan's mother could no longer live independently, Jan invited the family matriarch into her home. Her siblings thought the plan was perfect. Jan is the oldest child and a nurse to boot. Jan knew that it would be hard to have three generations under one roof, and she gave it a good try. But it just wasn't working. Her energy was drained, she was less effective at the hospital, and her relationships with her husband and children and even her mother suffered.

Against her siblings' objections, Jan placed her mother in a wonderful assisted living facility.

Everyone, including Jan's mother, was infused with new life. Jan maintained her role as family caregiver representing her mother's best interests as they negotiated medical and financial choices. She took on caregiving in a way that worked for her, and everyone benefitted.

Caregiving can feel like a standardized test. Many caregivers think that there are right answers, and they are desperate to get the best score possible. Some believe there is a book somewhere that offers these so-called right choices: Good adult children take feeble parents into their homes. Old people live in nursing homes because their children don't care about them. No one takes care of your family members as well as you can, so you need to count the pills and brush the dentures.

Unlike standardized tests, there are no right choices in caregiving. Like standardized tests, though, the task is designed so that no one will achieve perfection.

Here is the secret to caregiver success. **You don't have to be a perfect caregiver, just be perfectly you.** I first learned this lesson in my efforts to be a perfect parent. My parenting educator and coach, Barbara Swenson, offered the 51 percent rule. She says that if you are the kind of parent you want to be 51 percent of the time, love will do the rest.

Imagine two kids on a perfectly horizontal teeter-totter. If one child scooches back just a bit, gravity will take this child to the ground. Be the caregiver you want just a bit more than half the time, and love will take you the rest of the way.

You have what it takes to do this caregiver job. I promise that you will make mistakes. However, if you can get to the end of the day being the caregiver you want to be 51 percent of the time, love will take you to 100 percent. Many times this 51 percent does not involve doing something; you do it by simply being there.

While caregiving is hard for everybody, it's hard for different people in different ways. You have the best chance of getting to 51 percent when you know yourself, when you do what you do best, and when you get help from others with things that are hard for you. Hit 51 percent day after day, and you have a formula for caregiver success.

THE 51 PERCENT RULE TO CAREGIVER SUCCESS

If you are the person you want to be 51 percent of the time, love will do the rest and get you to 100 percent.

WHAT'S YOUR PAIN AND PLEASURE PROFILE?

On a Friday morning Maya learned her mother had a stroke. She wanted to be at her mother's hospital bedside, but what would she do about her son? She called her husband, who was out of town and asked if he could cut his business trip short.

This was not an option. "What am I going do?" she asked out loud. Her husband suggested, "What about Liz?"

Maya's husband had lost track of his distant cousin Liz when they were teenagers. They recently reconnected at a family wedding. Her seven-year-old son had instantly clicked with Liz's three sons.

Maya said to her husband, "I can't impose like that. I hardly even know Liz." Her husband encouraged her, suggesting Liz would be happy to help. Out of desperation, she picked up the phone and made the call. She told Liz what was happening and asked if her son could spend some time over at their house after school. Maya fell over herself with apologies, but Liz cut her off.

"I'm so glad you asked! This is perfect! My boys had been pestering me to invite your son over. This is a real treat for us! Why don't you head off to the hospital, and I'll pick your son up at school. Can he spend the night?" Liz said.

Maya was shocked. She knew that having an extra child at her house would have been hard for her, and she just assumed it was that way for others. She genuinely got the impression that this was easy for Liz. She felt a huge burden lifted from her.

You have always known that you cannot take on caregiving alone. Here's something that may be news to you. **While caregiving has its challenges for everybody, it's hard for different people in different ways.** Once you know what's easy for you, you can join forces with others who can easily do the things that are hard for you, like Maya did.

In general your life works best when you spend more time doing things that bring you pleasure and less time with things that bring you pain.

No two people draw the line between pain and pleasure the same way. Some people love shopping, and others would rather get a root canal than go to a mall. Some love hot spicy foods and diving out of airplanes and roller coaster rides while others wonder about the sanity of people who do those things.

You are wired to interpret whether any given experience brings you pain or pleasure.

You might just assume that other people are like you. If you don't like something, you assume that it's unattractive to other people, too. If you don't like to cook, for example, you may turn down your friend's offer to bring over a casserole. You might think it's too much to ask. Just because cooking is hard for you, it does not mean it's hard for everybody. Cooking may be a real joy for your friend who is grateful for a way to help a friend in need.

Even close friends and life partners can like and dislike different things. The only way you'll know whether something brings pain or pleasure—to both yourself and others—is to ask.

Action step: Start paying attention to the things in your day that bring you the most pleasure. Observe how often you assume other people are like you. You have a hard time talking with strangers, so you don't ask your outgoing friend to make calls to find the best surgeon for your cousin. You take pride in your clean, orderly house, and you somehow think less of your friend who organizes papers by deciding which pile of paper it joins. It's so easy to get organized, why not just do it? Consider what happens if you allow people to have a different pain and pleasure profile than you do.

WHAT ARE YOUR STRENGTHS AND PASSIONS?

When you shop for a car or a house or a plant, you learn the features valued by the typical buyer. The house has a water view. The car is both sporty and energy-efficient. The plant is interesting four seasons of the year.

For what are you known and valued? What are your strengths?

Surprisingly few people know what their strengths and gifts are. If you are one of them, here are a few exercises that can help you identify them. This will offer clues about which caregiving efforts best suit you.

- As you go about your days, consider whether the activity makes you feel more alive or more drained. You might even jot them down on a list you keep for a few weeks. Maybe you enjoy paying bills because you can see concrete results for your efforts. You might be the perfect person to make sense of the hospital bills and the insurance payments.

- Think about times in the past when time stood still. What were you doing? Gardening? Taking a walk in nature or through a museum? Cheering at a baseball game? Maybe you can take your adult nephew with Down's syndrome to a ball game and give the parents a much-needed rest.

- Reflect on the nice things people tell you about yourself. Maybe someone compliments you on a terrific job throwing a surprise birthday party or organizing a closet or playing piano. You might dismiss the comment and think, "That's no big deal. Anyone can throw a party!" You might be the perfect person to organize a fund-raiser to help your dear friend pay the huge medical bills.

Ideally you take on the tasks to which you're best suited and get the help of others for things that are hard for you. Many caregivers listen to that little voice in their head that tells them they're asking too much when they ask others to help with things that are hard for them; they don't want to impose on others.

Many caregivers are worried about imposing on others. They erroneously think that if running errands is hard for them, it's hard for others in the same way. Please remember that, for some people, running errands is effortless. Look for the person in your trusted inner circle who tends to live in the car. Say, "Next time you're at the store, could you pick up some Epsom salt?"

Once you know what your strengths are, you are in a better position to find a way to pitch in with care in a way that's easy for you. If you love to garden, you can weed grandma's yard. If you love to take on projects, you can seek out products and services that will help your ailing neighbor who has crippling arthritis. If you love the sense of accomplishment at looking at a clean room, offer to clean your mom's house.

The secret to successful caregiving turns on your ability to contribute from your strengths and gifts and enlist the help of others who contribute in areas where you are weak.

Action step: Ask friends and colleagues, "If you could only call one person for help, under what circumstances would you call me?" or "If I were on the cover of a magazine, what would the magazine be and what would the article be about?" Then look for opportunities to use your gifts.

If your gift is finding creative solutions to problems, keep your eyes and ears open for the times that call for a fresh perspective. You might be the perfect person to help during an emotion-packed conversation among family members—maybe about dividing caregiving duties when some family members live closer than others. You're the one who says, "Let's step back. You're assuming that Faith can't contribute because she lives so far away. Is there a way that she can help that does not require her physical presence? Can she hire someone to pitch in with cleaning instead of going to the house like you do?"

WHAT IS
YOUR TEMPERAMENT?

Caregiving comes with many big challenges: The pain of loss. The need to learn new things quickly. The need to make bold choices in the face of uncertainty. Giving up opportunities in the long run, and maybe vacation time in the short run. Short-circuiting your career. Spending your time doing something you need to do rather than what you want to do.

Your temperament—a collection of traits describing your innate response to any given environment or situation—suggests the times you will shine and the times you can use outside support. It includes things like your adaptability to change, the intensity of your emotional response, and your ability to tolerate uncertainty. Your temperament, like your height, is coded in your genes and modified slightly by childhood experience.

Here are a few temperament traits:

- Comfort when meeting new people
- Sensitivity to the environment
- Adaptability to change
- Energy level
- Comfort with unpredictability

- Distractibility
- Ease of making transitions
- Extroversion vs introversion (recharged spending time with others vs preferring to be alone)
- Easy going vs serious
- Emotionally stable vs passionately expressive with feelings

Your temperament works just like gravity. Life is easier when you make gravity and your temperament work for you. Working against your temperament is like riding a bike uphill; working with your temperament is like coasting on a bike downhill. Imagine two people in the days and weeks after a medical diagnosis, in which each day is different. The person who does best with a routine will find it much harder than the person who loves new challenges.

Some people are temperamentally inclined to feel most comfortable with people in certain age groups. Dana works well with every age group, but she lights up around babies. When her extended family gathered at the hospital to await news of the operation, Dana offered to stay at home with her siblings' kids. Her sister-in-law, who is temperamentally drawn to working with seniors, left her own infant with Dana so she could support her grandparents.

You may know people who shine under specific circumstances. Some professionals like surgeons and firefighters are wired to be calm under crisis. Other people live for parties even as young children. Jack, the chief of police in his town, got the first call when a tornado hit his parents' house. As a first responder, he made sure his parents were safe, found the family dog, and got them all to a shelter. His brother Pete, who is good with details, worked with the insurance company and contractors to organize the house repair. Their sister Jenny, who loves celebrations, threw their parents' fiftieth anniversary party.

ARE YOU WILLING TO BREAK RULES?

Your willingness to challenge the rules is part of your temperament. Sometimes the willingness to break rules allows you to find new ways to make your loved one's life better. Mia knew that her grandmother, now in late stages of dementia, always loved babies. Mia followed her impulse to bring her grandmother a doll, and the many happy hours her grandmother spent with the doll in her arms made Mia glad she did.

Your temperament is neither bad nor good. It just is. Any temperament trait can be either your strongest asset or your biggest challenge. Your life works best when there's a good fit between your temperament and the job at hand.

Esther said, "Ed is strong-willed. He grabs hold of an idea like a dog with a bone. I found this trait annoying. I would often say at the end of a heated discussion, 'Ed, just give it up.' His persistence looked much different when his never-give-up attitude helped get his brother the care he needed."

It's often easiest to collaborate with people who have similar temperament traits, whether it's someone you live with, care for, or share caregiving. Imagine two people making dinner plans. When both people like to try new restaurants, or both people like familiar places with familiar tastes, it's a short conversation. But when the person who wants a new dining experience tries to make plans with someone who likes going to one of three favorites, negotiation gets more complex.

WHICH TASK IS RIGHT FOR YOU?

Caregiving works best when you fit the right task to the right person. Here are a few examples of making good matches:

What is your preferred level of activity?

- If you like being on the go, your temperament is best suited to running errands, taking loved ones to medical appointments, taking the kids to the park.

- If you like staying at home, you will be happier playing cards with a loved one to give the main caregiver a break, or cooking or cleaning.

Do you get recharged by being around people or by spending time alone?

- If you like being around people, see if you can host get-togethers, organize a night out, or take the loved one to appointments.

- If you like time alone, you are best suited to mowing the lawn, shoveling snow, researching medical conditions, and filling out endless insurance forms and other paperwork.

How focused or distractible are you?

- If you are focused, you could be tapped to get to the bottom of insurance discrepancies, call about the computer glitches, and get copies of medical records.

- If you are easily distracted, then you're the one who could call your loved one once a week to ask, "How are you?" invite a caregiver for tea, offer a shoulder to cry on.

———

Temperament differences can be the source of conflict; however, you can make differences work for you. Anna's strength is finding new creative solutions; then she's ready for the next challenge. Her brother Mario does best when he's in his routine. Anna used to describe Mario as "difficult" when it came to managing the change in their father's health status; now she understands that there's nothing wrong with Mario. Rather, they're just different. They've divided their work up so that Anna's in charge when things are changing, and Mario's in charge once things settle into a routine.

If you and your loved one have different temperament traits, you can craft win-win solutions so both of you get what you want. If you are an extrovert caring for an introvert, get out and socialize. If you are the introvert and your loved one is an extrovert, get out of the house when the house is filled with visitors.

How do you Learn New Things and Make Choices?

When a loved one is sick, you will undertake a crash course in new medical ideas and participate in many choices. Your temperament suggests how you approach these tasks.

What's my optimal dose of information? Information is powerful medicine. It's also readily available with a mouse click. You will get the greatest benefit when you know your optimal dose. Not too much or too little, but just right. Do you want to know everything about MS? Do you feel overwhelmed with too much information? Shirley is an empowered patient, but when her doctor started telling her the side effects from the medication, she said, "Please stop. I'll get every one of those side effects. I trust that you're making the best choice for me."

How do I piece together the big picture? There are two basic styles:

Information-oriented: Do you put pieces of information together and let the large structure emerge, like building a house of cards? If so, you most likely work best with the details of one task at a time. "Let's get through the operation, then we'll talk about chemotherapy." You may feel lost or overwhelmed with the big picture.

Idea-oriented: Do you like the big picture first so you know where to hang the details? If so, you work best with people who give you a big overview before launching into details. "Treatment will involve an operation, followed by six rounds of chemotherapy then radiation." You may be confused with the details unless you have the big picture.

How do I learn? Everyone learns differently. How do you best learn? Imagine that you need to learn how to care for your loved one's healing incision.

If you are a visual learner, you may have slept through the lectures at school and purchased class notes. You learn best by reading, watching a video, and looking through pictures. You might learn about wound care best by reading tips on a Web site, looking at pictures in a brochure, or watching a video, even if the volume is off.

If you are an auditory learner, you may have skipped the class reading assignment, but you never missed a lecture. You learn about dressing changes the best when someone talks you through it, either by a medical professional or on a tape or CD.

If you are an experiential learner, you learn by doing. You might want someone by your side demonstrating how the bandage is placed and secured.

How do I make choices? Everyone makes choices differently. Let's say you're trying to decide whether to cut back your work hours so you can spend more time caring for your loved one.

Practical: You consider all the choices and identify which works best in your life. You might investigate all your options, including the local resources to piece together your caregiver plan.

Analytic: You calculate how choices add up. You might calculate the reduced income when you cut back on work hours and compare that with the additional expense for in-home care if you maintain your current work hours.

Intuitive: You identify the vision, then go with your gut. You might just have a hunch that it's time to work part-time.

People-based: You consider how your choice will impact the quality of relationships with people important to you. You might balance the impact on your coworkers if you cut back your hours against the impact on your family if you spend more hours at home.

HOW DO YOU NOURISH YOUR BODY AND YOUR MIND?

Peggy did her best to take care of herself. She ate well and exercised regularly. She maintained the eating habits she learned as a girl: three squares a day and no snacking. She usually had cereal for breakfast, a sandwich for lunch, and pasta for dinner.

Peggy got an email from an old friend who would be in town on a project. Could she take Peggy up on her offer to sleep on the couch? Peggy was delighted. She would be home recovering from an operation on her carpal tunnel, and she wasn't sure how she would manage with just one hand.

So Peggy's friend jumped in and took over the cooking, serving protein at almost every meal: eggs for breakfast, salad with sliced turkey for lunch, and fish for dinner. Then she set out snacks and encouraged Peggy to eat every few hours, reminding her that healing bodies need protein.

Peggy noticed how much better she felt, and it was more than just being freed from job stresses. Her body felt like it was running better; she was sure it was from the change in her diet. After her friend left, she modified her eating habits from a carbohydrate-rich diet to a protein-rich diet. She tries to eat salmon or other fish with omega-3 fatty acids several times a week. She finds that she can focus better when she eats every few hours. She has packets of almonds, raisins, and crackers in her car and purse. While most people feed hunger pangs, Peggy knows that she gets grumpy when she needs food. When she is annoyed, she's learned to consider when she last ate.

Albert wondered how much sleep the normal person really needs. He had a hard time turning off his computer, his TV, and his mind, and he tried to get by on about five hours of sleep a night. He started taking an afternoon nap and found this made a big difference.

Human bodies, like cars, need fuel to run. The things you eat, the time you sleep, and the effort you invest in connections with people and things outside of yourself fuel your caregiving efforts.

Many caregivers wonder, "What's normal?" If only they could find the book that offers the normal way to eat or the normal amount to sleep or the normal response to the stresses of caregiving.

The better questions are, "What's normal for me? How much do I need to sleep? How often do I need to eat? How much time do I need to spend with friends to be at my best?" Unfortunately, you did not come with an owner's manual; however, you can write your body's owner's manual by just paying attention to what works best for you.

Here are some tips that will help you write your own owner's manual.

Try shifting from the question, "What's normal?" to "What's normal for me?" when it comes to —

EATING

- What's your ideal meal frequency? Three squares a day? Grazing every two to three hours?

- What foods make you feel your best? How does your body react to protein, complex carbohydrates, and fat?

- Many find the glycemic index to be a valuable tool in choosing foods that work best for them.

- Do you know when you're hungry and when you've had enough to eat?

- Do you react poorly to certain kinds of foods? Food allergies can drain your energy.

- Do you drink enough water? If you wait until you're thirsty, you're already dehydrated. Dehydration zaps energy.

GREAT MEDICAL WORD: BORBORYGMUS

The sound that comes from under your shirt when you're hungry has another name besides a growling stomach. The fancy word that could become helpful in a Scrabble game is *borborygmus*. Physiologists say borborygmus is the sound of air that you swallow as it moves through your small intestines.

SLEEPING AND RECHARGING

- How much sleep do you need each night to feel refreshed?
- What hours are you most productive? Feel most alive?
- What activities make you feel recharged?
- What types of people make you feel recharged? Which personalities drain you?

NAPS AREN'T JUST FOR BABIES

If your loved one sleeps during the day, you may treasure that time. You can finally catch up on your chores without disruption or have a moment to hear your own thoughts. What would happen if you used that time to rest too? Many clinical studies show the health benefits of naps.

EXERCISING

- What time of day do you prefer to exercise?

- What kind of exercise works best for you?

- Do you do better with an exercise buddy or is your exercise time a chance to be alone?

- What's your exercise plan when your routine is disrupted by travel or the unexpected phone call? This is the time it's hardest to maintain exercise routines and the time exercise has the greatest value.

THE EXERCISE HABIT

Once you have a well-established exercise habit, you'll want to maintain it. It's not because you love to exercise; rather you love the way that exercise makes you feel. Let's face it. Some days you whittle down to the bare bones of what you have to do. Those are the days you really need to get some exercise. Not enough time for the full routine? Scale it back. A little exercise is a much better choice than no exercise. It's all too easy as one day without exercise begets another and another. Next thing you know, your new habit is exercise avoidance.

WHAT MAKES YOU FEEL LOVED, VALUED, AND CONNECTED?

I rushed through the grocery store, trying my best to get home on time. Which line would have the shortest wait? I selected my favorite check-out clerk, Bill, because I knew how efficient he was. I read a magazine, sensing the line was not moving as fast as I expected. I looked up and discovered why. Bill was interrupted by many customers on their way out of the grocery store. He greeted most by name. I saw warm smiles and several hugs.

When my turn came, I said, "Bill, it's obvious you're well loved. What's your secret?" He replied, "It's simple. Each morning when I get up I decide that I'll try to make every person who crosses my path a little better off."

I was embarrassed. Here I was, counting the moments. There he was, making each moment count.

Most caregivers are counting the moments. There just never seems to be enough time. Caregivers say their best days are filled with times they make moments count. They feel the free exchange of love with those close to them.

The most effective way to feel loved, valued, and appreciated is to give it away. Here are some tips.

What is your love language? Just as there are many languages spoken on the planet, so, too, there are languages of love—and they're not all about talking. Gary Chapman, PhD, describes love languages in his book *The Five Love*

Languages: How to Express Heartfelt Commitment to Your Mate. Here they are:

- **Words.** Nothing says, "I love you," like, "I love you." Messages like, "I'm glad you're in my life," "I'm proud of you," and "You're special" are treasures. If you're caring for your frail father who speaks this language, you can say, "I always appreciated the way you found time for just the two of us." You can say to a child, "You're really taking charge of your diabetes. Good job!"

- **Gifts.** People who speak this language treasure a physical token of love that can be seen or touched. It doesn't matter if the gift is big or small. Dan and his wife collect beach stones when they're on vacation. While his wife was recovering from her operation, he found a special stone to bring each time he went to the hospital.

- **Touch.** You may know people who light up with a warm hug or a caring hand on their shoulder. Many who grow old or manage illness are already touch-deprived. When touch is your love language, touch deprivation translates to love deprivation. If this is your loved one, be generous with your touches. Take their hand before you give them the medication. Give them hug coupons to redeem. Ask, "Are you getting enough hugs?"

- **Acts of service.** If the person for whom you care speaks this language, you're in luck! This is the love language of caregiving! Your life is filled with moment-to-moment opportunities for giving and receiving love. Making a meal becomes a way of saying, "I love you."

- **Time.** This may be the hardest love language for caregivers to speak. Unlike words or touches or acts of service, which are infinitely renewable resources, time is usually in short supply. In their efforts to make the most of limited time, doctors let patients speak for about fifteen seconds before directing the conversation; many doctors and caregivers think they do not have the time to listen and fear a story that goes on and on. However, if your loved one speaks this language, you may be surprised how little time is needed to convey your love. You may find you have an easier day if you just sit down together for a few minutes. Play a hand of gin rummy or hearts. Consider taking your loved one on errands. Talk in the car. Make a pie together.

We all have a natural tendency to speak in our own native love language. That works well when love is exchanged between two people who speak the same love language. You can exchange words or gifts or do nice things for each other.

Challenges arise when the giver and the recipient have unrecognized differences in love languages. Melissa lavishes words of love upon her sister for whom she cares. One day when Melissa was washing and brushing her sister's hair, something special happened. Her sister seemed happier and more settled. She realized that touch is her sister's love language. Even though Melissa is not big on hugs, she makes extra efforts to touch her sister.

If you find yourself giving and giving and giving, and it seems like it's never enough, consider a switch to a different love language. Giving love in a language the recipient does not speak is communicating to a foreigner when you don't speak the native tongue. Shouting will not solve the problem; switching languages or finding a translator is the solution.

Get to know your love language and the love language of those you care about. It will help you take better care of yourself. And start saying, "I love you," in the language the recipient best understands.

SAY "I LOVE YOU" OFTEN

Some say you can never be too thin or too rich; Frank says you can never say, "I love you," too many times.

Frank's wife recently lost a courageous battle with cancer. This devoted husband says, "I regret that I did not, often enough, tell my wife how important she was to me and how lucky I was to have her with me for more than fifty years. This was partially due to denial that her cancer would be terminal and partially due to the fact that I cannot tell her this after she is gone."

Marianne knows it's never too late to start saying, "I love you." This sixty-year-old woman drives four hours each way to care for her aging parents. For the first time, she sat down and asked her eighty-seven-year-old father to tell her stories about World War II. She learned her father fought on the beaches of Normandy! She says, "As my father walked me to the car, he told me for the very first time he loved me. I could hardly believe my ears."

What makes you know you're making a difference? Syd looked up at me with glassy eyes and asked, "Have I mattered? Has my life made a difference?"

I've had the great honor of being with patients, friends, and relatives in their last days of life. Most ask the same question: Is the world a better place in some way because I was here?

If you care for an adult, your loved one will most likely arrive at the end of life before you do. One day, though, you will look back and ask this all-important question. You can live today so that you have the answer you want when you get there.

Just like your body needs air, your soul feeds on the knowledge that you are making the world a better place. Different people use different yardsticks to measure their contributions. This yardstick is neither good nor bad; it just is.

CREATE TREASURED MOMENTS

Michael said, "It's a shame I won't hear what they say about me at my funeral. Why don't we say these things in life?"

You can! Tell people why they're important and how they've made a difference in your life. It's the perfect way to make a connection—to create memorable moments.

Each person makes a difference in a unique way. Maybe it's being the best parent you can be. Maybe it's writing a beautiful poem or feeding the hungry or solving a hard problem. In whatever form your contribution takes, the need to count is universal.

Here are the major measures of success:

YOU GET RESULTS

You experience success when you get things done and have evidence to prove it, like a stack of folded clothes, a clean room, or the knowledge that your aunt took all the medications as prescribed that day.

You experience setbacks when you can't get the desired results, like the failure to persuade your husband to give up smoking.

You can get back on track by identifying a task under your control, like getting a phone number for a smoking cessation support group.

FEEDBACK FROM OTHERS

You experience success when others comment on your contributions like being told by the doctor that you've done a good job with dressing changes to treat your father's infection.

You experience setbacks when you think you are being criticized. The doctor tells you to pay more attention to the corner of the wound at the next dressing change.

You can get back on track by remembering what you have done well and asking how to do it better. You can ask the doctor, "How am I doing with the rest of the wound? Could you show me exactly how you want the wound to be packed?"

Please note: when people offer a critique of your ability to take on a certain task, they are not judging your character. You're not a bad person. You can be a good person who has more to learn about wound management, for example.

YOU'RE PROVEN RIGHT

You experience success when you are right. The appointment is on Thursday, just as you remembered. The medication is taken twice a day, not three times a day.

You experience setbacks when you are wrong. The appointment is on Friday, not Thursday, as you had mistakenly written on the calendar.

You can get back on track by recalling all the times you have been right and jumping back into a new question in search of an answer. You can tell yourself that out of almost a hundred appointments, you've gotten it right 99 percent of the time.

YOU'RE PART OF A TEAM

You experience success when you are included. You're included in the conversation with the doctor about the next steps and your mother asks for your opinion.

You experience setbacks when you are excluded.

You can get back on track by seeing your role in the bigger picture. Maybe your aging mother asked you to step into the waiting room so she could discuss a private matter with the doctor. Your role in the team in this moment is to graciously respect your mother's right to privacy. Sometimes it's harder to contribute by not doing something than assuming a hands-on effort.

Every person you meet measures success in his or her own way. People give their best when they experience success. This includes your family member or your friend you support. If your mother measures success by her results, tell her, "Wow, you made it all the way around the block today." If your brother who thrives on being right makes a mistake, say, "Thank goodness you made a mistake. I was beginning to worry that you might not be human after all." If your child thrives on recognition, say on the phone with your child in hearing distance, "You are not going to believe what your daughter did. She drew a beautiful get-well card, addressed it, and sent it to a classmate who had a broken arm."

You can also ask for others to remind you of your successes in a way that's most meaningful for you. Say to your partner, "Could you please remind me what I actually accomplished this week?" or to your hospitalized friend, "Did you like the bouquet I sent?" or to your sick father, "How am I doing taking care of you? This is new for both of us."

What makes you feel connected to something bigger than yourself?

Successful caregivers get strength from a source outside of themselves. What connections remind you that you are not alone in the world and that you are part of something bigger than you?

- Your religious or spiritual practices
- Your family
- A community group
- Nature
- Art
- Music
- A mission
- A hobby
- A passion

Maintain regular connections.

WHAT IS YOUR PAIN PERSONALITY?

Marilyn says, "I don't understand why my husband makes such a big deal about blood draws. It's only a little poke!"

Marilyn's husband really does have pain with blood draws. Marilyn made a common mistake. She assumes that other people react the same way she would if she were in their shoes.

Just as each person has a unique thumbprint, so, too, each person experiences the pain from a blood draw or a broken bone or a broken heart differently.

Many caregivers think that the heart of their job is offering comfort to those in pain. You are best able do this when you understand that each person has an innate response to pain that is shaped by their wiring and their upbringing. The most effective caregivers tune into the response of the person who has the pain.

I have observed five patterns that I call the pain personalities:

The Strong Stoic takes pride in being healthy and being tough. Illness and weakness are shameful conditions, so they hide their pain. Strong Stoics often wait too long to go to the doctor.

The Worried Well, previously called hypochondriacs or maybe cyberchondriacs, see at least parts of themselves in any diagnosis, then conclude that they are afflicted. About one out of four office visits to the primary care doctor addresses the worries of the Worried Well.

The Ostrich uses denial to ignore the pain and pretend that things are fine. Like Strong Stoics, Ostriches wait too long to see the doctor. Denial is a part of many medical conditions such as eating disorders or alcoholism.

The Victim is someone for whom pain brings benefits they want to keep by hanging onto their pain. They say with words that they want to get better, but their actions tell a different story.

The Ideal Patient pays attention to the pain signals and responds with the appropriate urgency.

Lilly says, "That wedding vow to be there in sickness and in health sounds good, but it's not easy. My husband, Joel, took time from work to help me after my hysterectomy. One day I asked him if my incision looked infected; it seemed red around the skin staples. He snapped at me, 'Stop with the worries! The sky is not falling!' Then again, after his heart attack I snapped at him, 'How am I supposed to help you if you won't tell me when it hurts?!'"

Why the conflict between husband and wife who care deeply for each other? They have different pain personalities, and they are frustrated when the other responds differently than they would. Lilly, like others who have a Worried Well pain personality, tends to state the worries sooner and more often that the Ideal Patient would. Joel, like Strong Stoics, tends to stay quiet until long after an Ideal Patient will admit to pain. The snapping between them is really a statement, "Why can't you be more like me?"

Once you know your pain personality, you know what kinds of adjustments to make so that you don't wait too long to get medical attention, and you don't get overly concerned with every pain. Further, it helps you treat the person with the illness with more compassion. You can step into their shoes and see how they see the world, even when it's different from your own.

Action step: Identify the pain personality of those around you so that you can take the appropriate action when they are in pain. If your husband is a Strong Stoic, for example, and tells you about pain, you can tell the emergency room doctor, "This man never says a word unless the pain is severe." Know your own pain personality so you can adjust your response.

AN ALTERNATIVE WAY TO THINK ABOUT PAIN

If you're like most people, you would rather avoid pain. In fact, pain can seem like an enemy.

What if you thought of pain as a messenger? What if pain is an important part of your body's design that nudges you to action?

Pain is like your car's dashboard warning lights. It's designed to keep you safe, guide your actions, and optimize your health. Pain serves you by drawing your attention to something that's out of balance. The pain of a burned finger pulls your finger from the stove.

PAIN THAT IS NOT PHYSICAL

While caregivers most commonly respond to their loved ones' physical pain, they themselves most commonly experience emotional pain like sadness and guilt and anger. Both physical and emotional pain hurt. Both can lead to suffering. Both kinds of pain are calls to action.

Here are some dark pains that caregivers experience—and the message each form of pain brings:

Stress is a pain that tells you that you do not have enough. You might think that you don't have enough time or enough money or enough resilience or enough love.

Sadness is a pain that tells you that you have lost something such as a favorite pen or the chance to see a friend or relax Sunday mornings with the newspaper.

Guilt is a pain that tells you that there is a mismatch between the person you would like to be and your current thoughts, feelings, or actions. Nice people don't get angry at a sick relative, yet you feel guilty when you do.

Disappointment is a pain that tells you there is a mismatch between the world as you expect it to be and the world as it is. You followed every detail of the doctor's instruction, and the procedure didn't offer the relief from pain as you hoped and expected.

Anger is a pain that draws your attention to an unmet need or your threatened safety. Your brother made a sarcastic comment when you told him how tired you were.

What does this mean for you? If you feel guilty, or you're angry or you're stressed, it's like a warning light on your car's dashboard. Look for the reason that the alarm sounded. If you're sad, what have you lost? If you're guilty, what were you expecting of yourself that you did not deliver? If you're angry, what do you need?

PAIN IS A CALL TO ACTION

Pain hurts so you pay attention. It continues to hurt until something happens.

Some people manage pain by ignoring it. They think, "It will pass." Sometimes this works, but it's not without risks; ignored pain can lead to a more dangerous condition. The relief of pain is sometimes an ominous sign. For example, an inflamed appendix hurts; if it ruptures, the pain suddenly eases.

Sore muscles and backs will improve. They get better faster with rest.

When you have pain, ask, "What do I need to do?"

HOW DO YOU MANAGE STRESS AND GUILT?

Stress is part of the lives of caregivers. I see stress as a special pain delivering the message that there is not enough. It often seems like there's never enough time or helping hands or uncluttered surfaces or peace and quiet.

In general, you get stressed when you're spending too much of your time and energy in things that drain you and not enough time doing things that recharge you.

The solution is spending more time doing things that recharge you, spend less time with things that drain you, and make sure that you're fortified with nutrition for the mind, body, and soul.

Here is your three-step process to create a customized stress management program:

Step 1. Identify your stress triggers and make a plan to avoid them. Is there something that drives you nuts? Wet towels on the floor? A car with a near-empty gas tank? No milk in the house? Figure out a way to proactively avoid those situations.

Step 2. Recognize the early signs of stress. Where do you feel stress in your body? What are the early clues that stress is building? Does your voice go up? Do you snap at people? Forget where you put your glasses? Can you get someone to be your stress gauge? ("Martha, can you tell when I'm stressed? Could you give me stress scores?")

Step 3. Make a list of stress-busters. It could include activities like walking, dancing, meditation, calling a friend, or washing the dishes. Keep a copy of the list on the fridge and on your computer.

Guilt, like stress, can impair caregiving.

As she was driving to see her father, Maggie wonders what makes her feel more guilty: short-changing her dad or her kids.

A year earlier Maggie thought it was finally time to live her own life. One child was in college and another one would be off in a few years. Maggie had wanted to paint since she was a little girl, so she had signed up for a watercolor class at the community college.

Suddenly, her life unraveled. Her mother was diagnosed with cancer; she was gone in a few months. Her father said his final goodbye as he scooped a shovel of dirt on her casket, saying, "See ya soon, Toots."

Maggie wanted to do more for her father. Her parents had been lovebirds completely devoted to each other. Her father was a firefighter, and when he headed off for a fire, her mother would put the kids in the car and drive to the scene; she wanted to watch him come out of the burning building with her own eyes. Her father seemed lonely and lost after his wife's death.

Her daughter was floundering at college, and the counselor thinks she may have ADD. Her high-school-aged son just didn't seem right. He was sullen and spent much time in his room. She wanted to be more involved in his life and get to know his friends a little better.

Her husband commented about how irritable she had become. Maybe it's peri-menopause, she thought. She was feeling resentful that she didn't spend more time doing the things she loved, like painting. Then she felt guilty about feeling resentful.

Some days it seemed as if guilt drove her life. It certainly drained her energy. Some days she wished she could find a surgeon in the Yellow Pages who could cut out the guilt; she would feel liberated.

Maggie doesn't talk with any of her friends about her guilt anymore. They would just give her a lecture.

Guilt is a common feeling in the landscape of caregiving. Guilt can propel you to be the best you can be. Or it can immobilize you. Maggie would love to put on her magic caregiver cape. With her superpowers she would bring her mother back to life, help her daughter successfully sail though college, and see more smiles on her son's face. She would be less irritable. She wouldn't feel resentful when she had to put her paintbrushes down to respond to the crisis of the day. She and her husband would be more than cordial housemates.

You may have ideas about the person you would be if you had this caregiver cape. You could always be there for your loved ones. You would not get angry or resentful or say things you regret. You would never forget to make a phone call, make scheduling mistakes, or get caught in traffic.

Then there's the messy real world we live in. We're human, so we can't be all things to all people. We occasionally let people down. Sometimes it's out of necessity; we have to decide whose needs are most important at any given moment. We also make mistakes.

Guilt is the distance between the person you would be if you had that caregiver cape and the person you are in that moment. Even caregivers with the best intentions are subject to human frailties, no matter how much they love the person for whom they care. It's a rare caregiver who does not at some point or another feel angry or resentful. Almost everyone says things they later regret. There are so many details that a few are bound to be missed.

I would love to offer a magic tip for eliminating guilt from your life. I cannot. If you're the kind of person prone to guilt, your most effective strategy is learning how to manage guilt so guilt serves you rather than imprisons you.

Here are some tips for managing guilt:

Recognize the feeling of guilt. Nancy was late to a meeting with the social worker; traffic held her up. Intellectually she knew that she could not have prevented that midday accident on the bridge. Still she carried a nagging feeling all day about being late. Finally she recognized it to be guilt. Unrecognized guilt has a way of eating at your soul. When you just say, "I feel guilty!" it's like looking at the monster under the bed. Naming it can deflate it. Nancy could say to herself, "I don't have any control over traffic, and on most days I would have arrived early. "

Suspend your judgment of guilt. You would not make a judgment about a stomach ache, a sore shoulder, or a sore throat; there is no reason to judge guilt.

Look for the cause of the guilt. Guilt is a feeling that tells you that you are not acting like the person you want to be. Let guilt be a symptom or an alarm that alerts you to the belief about what you should do and what you really did.

Pat felt guilty about missing her son's basketball game. She took her mother to the doctor and they weren't done as soon as she expected. The root of the guilt is Pat's belief that good parents always attend their children's games. With the help of a parenting coach, she got some clarity about her parenting ideal. She wants to model for her child the importance of having a Plan B for when surprises emerge, help her son manage disappointment, and remind her son that she's in her son's corner rooting for him even when she's not physically there.

When you feel guilt, here is a trick that might help guide you to the cause. Replay the scene in your mind, but this time imagine it's a friend in your shoes. What would you ask this friend or tell this friend? Here are some lines that may apply:

"You are not Superman or Superwoman. You're just a person. You're allowed to make mistakes."

"You can't undo the past. And you can learn from the past to move forward."

Betty's husband was recovering from a heart attack, and she felt guilty because she gave in to her husband's request for frequent steak dinners. She did not cause her husband's heart attack by serving steak. Heart disease is complex. However, this is a good time to learn about heart-healthy eating.

It's normal to have dark feelings. You can have any feelings like sadness or anger that you would rather not feel. What do you need to do things differently next time?

Take action. Get your needs met. Offer an apology if needed.

Revisit your vision of the ideal you. You may still believe things that you learned as a child like, "Nice girls don't get mad." Sometimes your real thoughts, feelings, and actions are appropriate. In this case, the way to resolve guilt is to reinvent the ideal you.

Develop forgiveness. Forgiveness is the ability to let the past be just as it was without any need to change it. It's hard to do, but a skill well worth the investment.

Consider different choices for next time. Use this episode as a way to make a change for the better. Think about what you will do differently next time when you face the same circumstances.

2

KNOW WHAT YOU KNOW

Cassandra knew that her husband was just not the same after his heart bypass operation. Her husband's loss of interest in golf was worrisome, and his explanation of being too tired did not ring true. She thought he was depressed. She also knew that her husband thought depression was just a description of people with the character flaw. They lacked discipline.

One day Cassandra showed her husband a newspaper article about brain changes after open-heart surgery. She persuaded him to go in for an evaluation. Sure enough, he was clinically depressed. With successful treatment, he returned to his old self. That helped Cassandra return to her more balanced life.

You make choices based on what you know. Knowing what you knew used to be easy. There were facts and there were hunches. The facts—the things you read in books or heard from authorities—were true. Your hunches—the things your intuition told you—were suspect.

Not any more.

With information at your fingertips, you can see for yourself that the authorities often contradict each others' facts. The experts cannot even agree on a "simple" question like whether vitamins prevent cancer. How do you know what to trust and whom to trust? Your intuition—your small still voice—appears to be gaining importance in knowing what you know. Sometimes it can literally mean the difference between life and death.

The doctors told Meg her eighty-year-old husband had a serious case of the flu, but Meg thought something much more serious than the flu was going on. Three days later a CT scan proved Meg right. Her husband had a ruptured appendix. Had he been diagnosed promptly, chances are good he would have lived years after his appendectomy, but the delay in diagnosis cost Larry his life, despite the doctors' best efforts. Meg wonders what would have happened if she had stood up and insisted the doctors listen to her.

Here are some things to know that will help you make better choices that lead to a better caregiver experience.

KNOW WHAT YOU WANT

Some caregivers might think this is silly. Of course people know what they want! Yet, if you have ever reached out to a harried caregiver with the questions, "How can I help? What do you want?" you may have gotten a blank stare.

Or maybe you were the one giving a blank stare when someone asked, "How can I help you?"

In their well-intentioned dedication to their loved ones, some caregivers lose track of their own needs, much less their wants. They might not know what they want to eat, or how they want to spend a rare free Saturday afternoon, or what kind of support from a friend would bring comfort.

Like holding your breath under water, you can ignore your wants and needs for only a short amount of time. Just as the wisdom of your body will force you to the surface of the water, so, too, suffocated wants will be filled with unhealthy gasps of action like smoking or eating comfort food or one too many glasses of wine.

Children come into the world knowing what they want and when they want it. You don't need to ask them what they want for their birthdays; they'll let you know. Adults teach kids when it's appropriate to ask for what they want; however, some kids respond to this grooming by learning to ignore what they want.

Consider some messages kids hear when they ask their parents for what they want:

- "It's not polite." Adults tell children that good boys and girls don't ask for what they want.

- "No." Children learn that if they ask for what they want, they may not get it. Wanting comes with the risk of disappointment.

- "Don't be selfish." Adults tell children that nice people focus on the needs of others.

- "Don't be greedy." Adults convey the idea that there is not enough to go around, so if you get what you want, it could deprive someone else.

If you are one of those caregivers who has gotten disconnected from your wants, here are some tips to get reconnected.

- **Anticipate discomfort.** Asking yourself what you want may mean heading out of your comfort zone. You might even hear a parental voice in your head telling you that you are doing something wrong. Just say, "Thank you for that feedback. I'm trying something new, so I can be a better caregiver."

- **Start small.** As you get reacquainted with your wants, begin with little things. What do you want to eat? What kind of music would you like to listen to?

- **Manage loss and disappointment more effectively.** Nelson says, "I would rather just do without than know I want something I can't get. I hate being disappointed." For many people the most frightening part of knowing what they want is knowing and then not getting it. This is always a risk; however, you can learn skills that will help you manage the disappointment and loss more effectively.

- **Heal the "disease to please."** Giving with an open heart is a good thing, but, too much of a good thing—including giving—can be bad. People who harm themselves by their endless giving are sometimes called "people pleasers." Harriet Braiker, PhD, describes the "disease to please." Like any other disease, the illness places your health at risk. If you don't know what you want, you may be in its grips. Fortunately, the disease to please can be healed. The result is a better ability to give.

Action step: Let your imagination run wild for five minutes. If you could have anything you wanted, how would you spend your next birthday? What would you do for yourself next week or next month? There are absolutely no limits. Consider having fun with this as a family event.

ARE YOU BEING NICE
OR DO YOU SUFFER FROM THE DISEASE TO PLEASE?

We all want to be kind, giving people who make a difference in the world. In fact, giving can promote emotional and physical health. However, too much of a good thing can be bad for you. In fact, people pleasing can be dangerous to your own health.

Harriet Braiker coined the term "disease to please" in her book with the same title. She helps readers draw the line between giving that promotes your health and giving that threatens your health. She states that people with the disease to please

- Attend to others at their own expense
- Strive to be liked
- Avoid conflict
- Base their own value on their ability to make others happy

If this sounds familiar, consider reading *The Disease to Please*. Ultimately people-pleasing gets in the way of your ability to give. You can learn how to give in a different way through exercises in the book.

Imagine how much easier it will be for your family members and coworkers when you know what you want. They won't have to guess any more. They have a chance to bring a smile to your face. Plus, you are happier so you have more to give.

KNOW WHAT YOU WANT
BEFORE YOU SEE THE DOCTOR

Brenda noticed her father moping around the house and asked what was wrong. He said he was upset that he couldn't get into the yard and tend to his beloved roses. Why not, she asked? "My bum knee's acting up again." Brenda knew how much the roses meant to her father, so she persuaded him to make a doctor appointment.

Brenda was with her father during the appointment. The doctor quickly looked at the knee as he asked a few questions.

Then suddenly they were talking about everything except the knee. When the doctor abruptly got up and headed out of the exam room, Brenda asked, "But what about the knee?" The doctor shouted over his shoulder. "Take some aspirin." He was out the door before Brenda could ask the doctor about whether it was safe for her father to take aspirin. She had just read a study showing more Americans died from aspirin complications than AIDS. (This is true!) Brenda and her father left annoyed. They didn't fill the prescription for blood pressure medication the doctor handed them on his way out the door.

What went wrong here? Brenda wants to help her father achieve a personal goal of getting back into the garden. The doctor has a medical goal of diagnosing and treating medical conditions that could threaten his patient's life. A quick assessment told the doctor that the knee pain was caused by age-related arthritis, which did not pose any threat to this patient's overall health. The doctor went to other health concerns that were higher on his priority list, like blood pressure control and cholesterol levels.

The disconnect between patients' personal goals and doctors' medical goals can lead to problems for everyone. Brenda's father didn't get what he wanted and needed. Office visits like these may explain why only about half of patients take medication as prescribed.

MILK AT THE HARDWARE STORE?

Sometimes caregivers know just what they want, but they go to the wrong place to get it. They want a shoulder to cry on and go to a friend who will try to fix things instead of listen. Author and life coach Cheryl Richardson would say this is like shopping for milk at the hardware store. When you know what you want, go to the place you know you're going to get it!

When you are the patient, you are much more likely to get what you want from the doctor if you know in advance what you want. Here are three questions to consider:

1. What is your medical mission statement? If you had a slogan that guides your use of the health care system, what would it be? Here are a few:

- If it ain't broke, don't mess with it.
- Worry my way to health.
- Alive at 105.
- Just make the *&%$ pain stop.
- Enjoy each day to the fullest.

What's yours?

2. What is your personal goal behind your medical goal? Chances are good that you do not take cholesterol medication to hang your excellent lab results on the fridge. You have some personal goal that will help you do what you need to do to achieve your medical goals. Do you want to see your grandkids marry? Take a cruise? Go out for walks each morning?

3. What is your goal for this doctor appointment? Here are the most common reasons patients see their doctors. If you know what you want ahead of time, you have a better chance of leaving the appointment satisfied.

- To find out what's wrong. A diagnosis that finally makes sense of things brings a sense of relief.

- To get your questions answered. You may have questions that will guide your treatment or influence your day-to-day choices.

- To make a plan to move closer to your personal goals. You might want an idea about when you will get back to the golf course or the garden.

- To get relief from the symptoms. You may want to change pain medication or avoid treatment side effects.

- To know that you are not alone. Telling your story to a caring listener makes you feel better. The healing power of storytelling is often undervalued and overlooked.

When you are a patient advocate, chances are good that you visit doctors as someone who is in the patient's corner.

When you function as an advocate for your family or friend, you may want to

- Make sure the doctor knows the full truth. Maybe your parent is not taking medication as prescribed.

- Ask the doctor to clarify the treatment plan. You may think the doctor wants your partner to begin walks now and your partner thinks it's not for another three weeks.

- Ask for the doctor's help in following orders. You may ask for some help in making your child's dressing changes less painful or avoiding nausea.

- Make sure that your loved one's true concerns are being addressed. Your friend may complain to you bitterly about a side effect and then not bring it up with the doctor.

WHAT IS A PATIENT ADVOCATE?

When you think "patient advocate," do you think of adversary? Someone who puts on boxing gloves and goes a few rounds with the doctor?

How about thinking of a patient advocate as someone who puts on the team jersey and joins the players on the field? You can do this in the spirit of collaboration.

KNOW THE MOST COMMON FANTASIES ABOUT YOUR DOCTORS' POWERS

Wouldn't it be great if doctors had super-human powers? Many patients wish their doctors were part of their own medical fairy tales.

For those of you who want to replace the fantasy with truth, here are some things to consider.

- **Doctors are not mind readers.** Your doctors don't know what you think or how you feel. You must tell them. If, for example, your husband's biggest concern about the upcoming operation is the choking sensation from the breathing tube, encourage him to speak up! At the very least, the doctor can tell your husband what to expect; maybe your husband won't even need a breathing tube.

- **Doctors don't have crystal balls.** You may long to know what the future holds. What will it be like for your brother to get the chemotherapy? Will Dad be able to walk again after the stroke? How long will your father live? The doctor may say things like, "At this stage of disease there is a 70 percent five-year survival." As one of my patients said, "I'll either be 100% alive or 100% dead in five years. Now which is it going to be?" Regretfully, the doctor cannot answer.

- **Doctors don't know everything.** Medical knowledge is advancing at an exploding rate, so no one person can keep up with everything. You may know more about your sister's medical condition than your doctor does!

- **Doctors don't have "The Answer."** When your family faces a medical choice, there is no right answer. There's an answer that is best for your loved one at that time in his or her life under those conditions.

- **Doctors don't have magic wands.** The miracle drug that offers a cure without any risk simply doesn't exist. Make sure you know the possible risks before you agree to any treatment for someone you care for, including herbal remedies and nutritional supplements. And be suspicious of any product that claims to offer a cure for a wide variety of illnesses.

- **Doctors spend a limited amount of time with you.** Most doctors are employed by clinics or hospitals, and they're expected to meet productivity goals defined by their employers. That means your doctor is expected to see a certain number of patients each day and spend a limited time with each patient. Frequently it does not seem like enough time—to you, to the patient, and to your doctor. Prepare for the appointments so you can make the most of the time you have. Write a list of questions. Ask for a longer appointment when needed, even if it means paying for the time out of your pocket.

- **Doctors make mistakes.** The Institute of Medicine estimates up to 98,000 patients died in the hospital in 1999 as a result of preventable medical errors. That was ten years ago, and the estimates haven't changed. That's more patients than died from car accidents or breast cancer in the same year. Medical errors represent the eighth leading cause of death in the U.S. This isn't about bad doctors. Mistakes happen because the health care system is complex, health care is delivered by people and people make mistakes. The title of the Institute's report is *To Err Is Human*. Proactive and vigilant participation in heath care is your best protection. The caregiver plays the role of patient advocate.

- **Doctors are people too.** Doctors get angry, sad, and frustrated just like you do. And it may have nothing to do with you. A doctor who seems impatient might be thinking about the critically ill patient in the ER. A doctor who asks you the same question twice may have just received a worrisome call from a family member.

- **You have a job too.** As the family caregiver, you are often the person who helps make the medical plan happen. You are the person doling out the pills or taking your father to physical therapy. Think of this plan as a verbal contract. Let your doctor know if the plan isn't working and renegotiate.

KNOW WHEN TO BREAK THROUGH DENIAL

We don't see things as they are,
we see them as we are.

~Anais Nin

You might notice weight loss or a failing memory or increased alcohol consumption in your friend's parents sooner than you would in your own. It's often hardest to see unpleasant realities clearly when you're dealing with people you love.

Denial is a natural and necessary human defense. Who could read the morning paper and continue with the day without the ability to ignore or forget the pain in the world?

Family caregiving brings you in contact with some of life's most frightening and painful truths we all work the hardest to deny. Your parents will not live forever. You cannot protect your loved ones from pain, despite your best efforts. There is no way to protect yourself from losses. One day you, too, will die.

Denial can also be a barrier to the life that you want for yourself and those you love. Denial of the painful realities keeps you from taking action. Barry wishes that he had taken the car keys away before his father drove into the closed garage door putting his foot on the accelerator instead of the brake.

You know how much energy it requires to pretend you don't know something. It's like holding a beach ball under water. The minute you let your guard down, the ball bounces up.

It will just remind you of something you already know to be true. In the end, it's easier to admit the truth than deny it.

SAD BUT TRUE:
ALCOHOLISM AND DEPRESSION IN SENIORS

You visit an elderly family member who's confused or forgetful or listless. You might write this off to natural aging. However, alcoholism or depression might be the real reason. Grief, loneliness, and a loss of purpose can trigger alcoholism or clinical depression for the first time in senior years. Both depression and alcoholism can be successfully treated at any age. First, though, they must be diagnosed.

KNOW IF YOU'RE DEALING WITH THE PRESENT OR THE PAST

If you think you're so enlightened,
go spend a week with your parents.

~Ram Dass, spiritual teacher

Lisa says, "My father is in a panic about money, and it doesn't make any sense. Even after his 401k became a 101k, there's still plenty of money. The other day my father told the story about a favorite uncle who left a five dollar bill under the sugar bowl each visit during the Great Depression. Many times this money meant the family would not go hungry. Suddenly I realized that my father was not reacting to what's happening today; it's almost like he's reliving the Great Depression today."

Therapist Cathy Thorpe explains how and why the past influences our experiences in the present moment. Cathy sees human development as if she were looking at the rings of a tree. She points out that trees grow and develop by building on the growth of earlier years. So, too, our ability to respond to thoughts, feelings, and life challenges is built on earlier lessons.

Our responses and actions are not always those made by someone living in the outer-most ring with access to the wisdom and skills based on life experience. Think of the adult who has temper tantrums!

We revert back to behaviors from our inner, earlier rings when the circumstances are similar to painful events from our past. Even a wise, financially-secure senior can become the frightened, hungry eight-year-old who lived through the Depression.

Scott was sixteen when his gravely ill mother was airlifted to a medical center 200 miles away. The next day, he and his older sister drove as fast as they dared to reach the medical center. They ran into the huge hospital, searching for the room number he had been given. When they reached the room, they found a freshly-made bed. "Where is my mother?" he asked the nurse in the hallway. "Oh, she died," the nurse stated and walked away. Today, Scott, in his fifties, still dreads hospital visits, which colors his caregiver experience.

Here are some clues that you might be reacting to the past rather than to the present:

- You are told by someone you trust that you are over-reacting.
- Your intense emotions seem to take over.
- Your reaction doesn't fit the circumstances.
- Your emotion seems wrong or different than the circumstances call for.
- You have a hard time making simple decisions.
- You feel out of control at unexpected times.

If you find yourself feeling cornered, unable to see your choices and options, consider the possibility you are reacting to your past. Go back and see if you can find the situation that's triggered your reaction. Then remind yourself that you are not a child; you're an adult with adult resources. This simple exercise often breaks the spell of the past.

ENDING SIBLING CONFLICT
FOR CHILDREN OF ANY AGE

If you and your adult siblings start bickering like children, you are not alone. Many adults relive old sibling rivalries as they care for aging parents. Here's the good news. You are adults now, and you can put an end to old childhood fights for good. To get you started, here are the kinds of fights kids have.

- Jealousy fights. Children fear losing the parents' love to a sibling's; adults understand that there is plenty of love for everyone.

- Frustration fights. Children expect more than they get; adults possess skills that help manage disappointment.

- Dominance fights. Children need to establish superiority; adults can be different and equal.

- Entertainment fights. Children use fights to get attention or stave off boredom; adults can ask for what they want.

KNOW IF YOU'RE DEALING WITH SOMEONE IN YOUR CORNER OR JUST A PRETENDER

Caregivers form a web of connections with others. In the ideal caregiving world, your actions rise from your intention to promote the best interests of your loved one, and the people who help you have your best interests at heart.

It doesn't always work this way. You may know people who say they're acting to promote your best interests, but their actions say that they don't care about you as much as they care about themselves.

Katie says, "A coworker called regularly when I was with my son at the hospital. She said she was just calling to offer her support and see what she could do. After a while I realized that she was really calling to figure out when I would be back to work. She wasn't there for ME; she wanted to know when I would be back there for HER. That was a totally reasonable question. I just wish she had been more honest."

You life is easier when you know who is in your corner and who is just pretending to be. Or, as Dorothy in the *Wizard of Oz* might ask, are you dealing with a good witch or a bad witch? Good witches use their power to make the world a better place. Bad witches use their power to make a better place for themselves, often at the expense of others.

If you're a caregiver, chances are good you're dedicated to advocating for your loved one's best interests, and you want to believe that others are too. Some caregivers want to believe it so much that they ignore the signs that suggest otherwise.

Here are some ways that lead to bedeviled caregiving:

Pretenders who act as if they're in your corner. The newspaper is filled with stories about bad witches—scam artists who prey on the elderly and the vulnerable. Some are so slick that you don't catch on until the damage is done.

Sometimes it's more insidious. Look very carefully at anyone trying to sell you something and ask whose interests are served—yours, the vendor's, or both. Ask for the evidence that the product or service will help you. If this product supports or promotes health, clinical studies offer more compelling proof than testimonials.

Someone in your corner who makes mistakes. Caregivers maintain a precarious balance between self-interests and the best interests of their loved one. These two can come into conflict in small and big ways. In the most dramatic case, your loved one is ready to die, but you're not ready to let go. When the line is blurred, a simple statement like this can help: "This is hard for all of us. Let's get back to our priorities; we've decided we're here to support Mom's choices."

WHEN DOCTORS ACT OUT OF SELF-INTEREST INSTEAD OF THE PATIENT'S INTEREST

There is nothing quite as confusing as a doctor acting out of self-interests rather than the patient's best interests. It feels like the ultimate betrayal. Let's say you had an attentive, caring surgeon, but the surgeon was cold and distant after the operation when the widespread cancer extinguished hopes of cure. Here's why. In their minds, successful doctors cure patients; they feel like failures when they cannot. When they act out of self-interest, they avoid patients who have complications or elude cure because they're human, and all of us want to avoid the pain of personal and professional failure.

Pretenders acting like pretenders. This is the group of people whose words say that they are acting out of love, but their actions say that it's all about them. Even though this group of bullies and perpetrators of verbal and emotional abuse make up about 20 percent of the population, they cause about 80 percent of the interpersonal conflicts.

Sometimes you can spot them a mile away. The bad witches who do the most damage are those you don't see for what they really are. They would like you to believe that *you* are the problem. The truth is that they are both the source of the problem and the person telling the lie that it's about you. They are so convincing that you come to believe it.

Here are some things that bad witches—or even a good witch on a bad day—can do:

- Tell you how you should be feeling: "Come on. This isn't so bad."
- Tell jokes at your expense
- Accuse or blame: "This is all your fault."
- Demand or order: "I said this conversation is over."
- Call you names: "You're just being selfish."
- Give you the silent treatment
- Place unreasonable demands and expectations on you: "I don't know why you can't take Dad to the VA for his appointments every week."
- Criticize or judge: "Mom's got cancer and you want to EXERCISE?"
- Threaten: "If you don't lighten up, I'm out of here."
- Humiliate
- Slam doors, drive recklessly, yell
- Refuse to be pleased

When you're around these kinds of witches, you can feel as if you're walking on eggshells. Or as Sam Horn says in her book *Tongue Fu,* "You're talking on eggshells." You can come to doubt yourself, have a funny feeling in your gut, and begin to feel a little crazy. Your life can be miserable and confused if you do not see that these are not good witches as they would like you to believe; they're bad witches in disguise.

Sometimes the stresses of caregiving help you recognize bad witches for who they really are. Their insidious behavior becomes more obvious.

You do not have to live with bad witch behavior. Even if you have a lifelong relationship with a relative who treated you in disrespectful ways, you have the power to put an end to this behavior. The simple process of identifying someone as a bad witch means that you are over halfway to the solution. You can make new rules.

What do you do when someone who harmed you in the past needs care?

Imagine a child abused by the parent who is supposed to keep them safe. It could be verbal or emotional or even sexual abuse. Now imagine this child as an adult when this same parent is in need of care. What would you do if you were the abused child?

The answers are as varied as the families.

Whatever happened in your past, you deserve a life free of abuse today. As a child, you did not have much control over the way adults treated you; as an adult, you do. Even if you're 60 years old, you can decide to deal with parents in a new way. It is not easy. It will feel uncomfortable to set personal boundaries by saying things like, "Mom, no name-calling."

Or "Dad, stop telling jokes at my expense." Or "Let's talk, not yell."

Joshua says, "I hated my dad for what he did to me. I always thought normal parents fed their kids love and acceptance; we grew up on a steady diet of hatred and disdain. I spent most of my adult life trying to NOT be like my father. My brother told me I was crazy, but I decided to take care of my dad after his stroke. I had to let go of my hatred. The big surprise for me is how much I benefitted. Right before my dad died, he told me something I had wanted to hear my whole life. He said, 'I'm proud of you.' I never would have heard those words from my father if I had not made the choice to forgive him."

Caregiving is forgiveness in action. Some say perpetrators of abuse against vulnerable children cannot and should not be forgiven. I will not argue. Those who make the choice to forgive say that when you forgive, you free yourself from the bonds from the past. Forgiveness is not something you do for the other person; it's something you do for yourself.

KNOW THE DIFFERENCE
BETWEEN DOING AND BEING

To be is to do. Kant
To do is to be. Camus
Doo bee doo bee doo. Sinatra

~Bathroom graffiti

Imagine an intimate couple bickering. He thinks, "Why won't she just get to the point?" She thinks, "Why won't he listen?" He's at his best when he fixes things and feels drained going over and over a problem that has no solutions. She's at her best when she feels connected and feels drained when she feels alone. Their differences are sources of both the couple's strength and the couple's conflicts. He wants her to be more like him; she wants him to be more like her.

Did you see a scene in a marriage counselor's office? This same dynamic unfolds between doctors and patients, and between caregivers and their loved ones. While this is described as the classic conflict between a man and a woman, it can also be understood as the collision between two mindsets: the *being* mentality and the *doing* mentality. The doing mentality is about fixing and conquering and mastery. The being mentality is about connecting and caring and nurturing.

Caregiving requires both doing and being. A wise caregiver knows when it's time for doing and when it's time for being. While every person knows how to be and how to do, men and fathers and doctors have a reputation for doing, and women and mothers and nurses as being. As a female surgeon, for example, I shifted from being into doing.

A family caregiver in the doing mentality plows through the to-do list. A caregiver expressing the being force often becomes the most cherished member of a loved one's trusted inner circle because the loved one simply wants companionship.

The primary fear of a doing mindset is the fear of failure; the primary fear of the being mindset is abandonment. Caregiving means facing both fears. Imagine the anguish of the caregiver with a doing mindset who fails to help loved ones find a cure. Imagine the anguish of the caregiver with a being mindset who will face the ultimate abandonment that death brings. Both do-ers and be-ers run the risk of burnout.

Those caregiving with a doing approach avoid burnout by reframing what it means to win. While there may not be a cure for cancer, a loved one could enjoy more hours of freedom from pain and comfort. *That* is an achievable goal. Most caregivers support loved ones who are on a steady decline that will end in death. Caregivers who express a being approach can avoid burnout by investing in relationships with people who will be there after the loved one is gone.

Doing caregivers provide things that loved ones need; being caregivers provide the things that loved ones want. Some families call on one person to fix things and another to provide connection and comfort. A doing sibling, for example, might organize the insurance records and put the pills into the daily pill keeper. Another who lives 1,200 miles away might be the being caregiver and call the parent every night and just listen to the same stories over and over. Loved ones need both. Sometimes one person contributes both. In this case, it's important to discern what is needed in any moment.

3

DO WHAT
YOU NEED TO DO

I want to help my mother live and die
on her own terms.

~Sherry, a family caregiver

If Sherry had her way, her widowed mother would move
into an assisted living community; her mother wanted to
stay in her own home. Sherry is doing everything she can to
keep Mom at home, including hiring a companion to come
in a few days a week. She spoke the words in the hearts of so

many caregivers: "I want to help my mother live and die on her own terms."

Your ability to care for others, though, is contingent upon your ability to care for yourself. Sherry hired the companion not only to take her mom to physical therapy and the grocery store (tasks Sherry hates to do), but to give her mom some companionship to break the isolation of living alone. It also frees Sherry to continue to work full-time and even attend her much-needed YMCA exercise classes.

Bob learned a tough caregiving lesson the hard way. His mother was the primary caregiver for his terminally ill father. Bob regularly offered his mother a helping hand. She would smile and say, "No thanks. I'm fine." He expected his father's death, but he was devastated when his mother died before his father. Bob wondered if his mother would still be alive if he had pushed harder to share the caregiving burden.

You are constantly balancing many wants and needs that can pull you in different directions. Here are some ideas to help you organize your to-do list in a smart way that will help you look back without regrets.

BECOME THE PACK LEADER

Lord, please help me to be the person
my dog thinks I am.

~Bumper sticker wisdom

Cathy's mother required round-the-clock care when she moved in with Cathy, her husband, and three children. Cathy says, "Our family goes to church every Sunday. It's just something that defines us as a family. My mother didn't want us to leave and had all sorts of excuses, including concerns about the expense of hiring a home care worker. I knew that our family could not afford to give up this spiritual sustenance." Cathy remained steadfast in her commitment to her family's Sunday ritual despite her mother's displeasure. She knew this family time would make her a more effective caregiver.

Other caregivers in Cathy's shoes might have made the mother's comfort and pleasure the top priority, no matter what sacrifices it meant for the rest of the family. The family would be led by the mother's needs. This approach can work for short periods of time; however, in the long run it leads to burnout.

Cathy is clearly a strong family leader who looks out for the best interests of the whole family. Her only regret as she looked back is that she did not make time to go on dates with her husband.

How do you become a successful family leader? Cesar Millan, the dog whisperer, may offer a roadmap in his book *Be the Pack Leader*. That's right—caregiver as pack leader. Cathy is her family's pack leader.

Dogs in the wild are led by a single alpha dog. The leader is not always the biggest or strongest; it's the dog with the strongest calm, assertive energy. The pack leader sets the emotional tone for the group. A good pack leader helps others in the pack work together in a positive way. Through the alpha's strong leadership, the pack's best interests are promoted.

The dog whisperer helps families who think they have a problem dog. In most cases he believes that the problem is that the dog has assumed pack leadership. And the solution is the transfer of leadership from the dog to the human. Similarly, caregiving works best when the caregiver, and not the care recipient, leads the pack.

Here are some thoughts that will help you think about your leadership role, whether it's leading canines or humans.

Put the pack first. Dogs in the wild begin their days with walks; most humans like to begin their day with coffee and the newspaper. As a pack leader who puts the needs of the pack first, the human takes the dog out for a walk first and then drinks coffee when they return home. Similarly, successful family caregivers put their loved ones' needs first—and then attend to their own.

John says, "I used to go over to my parents' house and try to charge through my to-do list. Then I realized that my mom didn't share my priority for shoveling the driveway and getting the light bulbs changed. What was most important for her was sitting down and catching up over a cup of tea. Our visits work much better when I sit down with her for five minutes, then do what I think is important."

Maintain a strong, assertive energy. Imagine the human with a dog who is aggressive with other dogs. The human's anxiety about the dog's aggression compounds the problem. As the dog senses fear, she steps in to act as the alpha, and that leads to even more aggression. The solution is for the human to walk with authority and confidence instead of giving in to fear or anxiety.

Caregivers often face circumstances that elicit fear and anxiety. Hazel says, "My husband used to set the emotional thermostat in our family. Now that the dementia is taking hold, he's in a hot, angry mood much of the time. I learned that I can change the thermostat to my own happier mood. I used to catch my husband's mood; now sometimes he catches mine."

Strong family leaders are able to stay calm and centered during emotionally turbulent times. They can be in the presence of pain or sadness or anger without being overtaken by the feelings themselves. They maintain hope and optimism and inspire others in the family and community to do the same.

The leader understands the needs of each pack member. As a leader, your loved one's needs are front and center. However, there are other members of the family who have needs that must be addressed. The leader performs ongoing juggling.

Kate says, "After my brother-in-law Bob's accident, I organized around-the-clock family shifts at the hospital so Bob would never be alone. After a very long Friday night at the hospital, I drove home imagining how wonderful it was going to be to crawl into my cozy bed.

"I walked in the door, and my five-year-old threw her arms around me, and said, 'Let's play our game.' Every day we played a drawing game for ten minutes. It was our ritual that kept us connected. I realized that Bob was not the only one who needed my care and attention. I needed to do the little things that told my husband and kids they were important, even when I spent so much time away from them."

The leader sets the boundaries. A growl or a nip from the pack leader reminds wayward puppies that certain behavior is unacceptable. Family caregivers can set limits on unacceptable behavior too.

Tina says, "I told my brother in a wheelchair after his stroke that I understood why he was angry; however, I would no longer tolerate him yelling at me. If he raised his voice, I would leave." Pack leaders set and reinforce limits and boundaries not with anger but rather with their calm, assertive energy.

The leader inspires the rest of the pack. All dogs—even lone wolves—need their packs. Many family caregivers act like lone wolves, assuming all the responsibility falls on their shoulders. The strong pack leader is able to find a way for all family members to make a contribution.

Debbie says, "My work just happened to bring me back to my home town. Then Dad had his heart attack. I knew I couldn't care for Dad all alone. I could certainly be the quarterback, but I needed the whole team. I figured out a way for everyone to contribute. Even the grandchildren had a job. They learned new knock-knock jokes to keep Dad smiling."

Transition to a new pack leader is not always easy. Sometimes the family caregiver is already the identified pack leader. However, many family caregivers find themselves in a family leadership role for the first time.

Andrew says, "My father always made the family decisions and commanded respect. How was I going to take away his car keys in a way that let him preserve his dignity?"

The transfer of leadership may well be one of the biggest challenges of family caregiving. How do you care for aging parents or a life partner who are established family leaders? In the movie *The Godfather,* leadership was consciously passed to the next generation. Your loved ones may resent the circumstances that required them to relinquish power. When LBJ left the White House, he ran his ranch like a mini country on a smaller scale. You can find ways to let your loved one assume leadership in all parts of their lives they can still manage.

The rewards surpass the challenges. Dogs are happier and families are more balanced when the human acts as a strong leader who puts the needs of the pack first. The same thing happens with caregivers who offer strong family leadership.

WHAT DOES YOUR LOVED ONE WANT?

- They want to be valued.
- They want some control.
- They want to leave a legacy.
- They want to find a way to give.

Conducting difficult conversations. Successful pack leaders initiate difficult conversations. It might involve

- **Conveying bad news.** Telling your children a grandparent has cancer.

- **Navigating a change.** Creating a plan now that your partner who was the main breadwinner cannot work because of disability.

- **Resolving a conflict.** Confronting your sister who makes hurtful comments.

These conversations that are trying under any circumstance are particularly challenging when the health of someone you hold dear is on the line. Emotions run high, and the conversation hits close to home. Someone could get hurt when you raise the issue; however, someone will get hurt if you don't.

Here are some ideas that may help:

Sugar-coated bad news is still bad news. Peter says, "My wife got mad at me when she heard that I hadn't told her the whole truth about the biopsy results. I told her I was just trying to protect her. She said, 'You're not protecting me. You're protecting YOU. You can't stand it when I cry.' She has a point. I will do just about anything to avoid making people feel sad or disappointed. Sometimes this means keeping secrets or glossing over the dark cloud and getting right to the silver lining. By the time they really understand what I'm saying, I'm usually out of there. I know my wife and kids are strong, and they can handle it. I need to figure out how to deal with my own discomfort."

Strong pack leaders know that they can manage when people around them feel their feelings. They can deliver bad news with the full understanding of its expected impact on people they love.

Sugar-coated news smacks of deception. In the end, the kindest approach is the straight delivery.

Recognize you're having a conversation you would rather not have. Say, "Kids, I wish we didn't need to have this talk. You know things have changed with Grandma, and all of us need to make changes to make sure we take good care of her."

State the problem, and collaborate on the solutions. Many leaders think they have to deliver a complete solution when they present the problem. Maggie said, "I knew the time had come for my mother to move in with us, but I hated to ask the kids to share a bedroom. I thought about the options and delivered what I thought would be the best plan. When I finally told the kids, I was surprised. They already seemed to know the news. Further, they had a terrific plan I never considered. The kids turned the basement into their living suite. My mother moved into one bedroom, and we moved the TV from the basement to the other bedroom."

People are more likely to go with plans they help create. If you are making choices that involve other people, ask for their input. Even small children come up with terrific ideas. As the pack leader, you have the final say. However, you're leading the pack to a place they want to go.

Focus on the outcome, not the person. Tom says, "My sister gives me a hard time about the money I spend on the home companion for Dad. It's just a few hours a week, Dad likes the company, and it makes my life easier. My sister has no idea what it's like around here; she only sees Dad every few months. She tells me I should stop being selfish, give up a golf game and spend those hours with Dad. To be honest, I think the problem is that she wants her kids to inherit Dad's money I'm spending on Dad."

Ouch! What a tangled mess. Here's how they resolved the conflict. They focused on the outcome they were trying to achieve. They agreed that they wanted their father to enjoy a reasonable quality of life. They agreed that they were both responsible for their father. They recognized that they made different contributions because of their difference in physical proximity. They brought in a family friend to place the deciding vote when they disagreed about money.

Tom says, "A buddy on the golf course offered an idea that really helped make peace with my sister. He told me that I was not a mind-reader. It was not fair to assume I knew my sister's intentions when she made comments about how Dad's money is spent."

Listen. When you are in conflict, it's helpful because two people have a different point of view. Before you offer yours, try to understand theirs.

DELIVERING BAD NEWS

The job of delivering bad news often falls on the shoulders of the pack leader. They put their own pain on hold as they make plans and offer comfort to others. Their strong, assertive presence helps others find their own strength and courage. Later, they deal with their own pain.

I dreaded delivering a dire diagnosis as a practicing surgeon. How do you tell patients in the prime of life and their family members about a life-threatening illness? It's equally as difficult when it's your own family.

What would you say to family members if you needed to communicate the news of a serious illness? For example, your husband asks you to call his parents who live across the country and tell them about his prostate cancer diagnosis. Maybe your father was cleaning the gutter and fell off the ladder, breaking a hip. Consider if a favorite aunt has decided it's time to stop fighting. How do you deliver bad news?

Decide who needs to know first. Life partners, children, and parents are usually on the list.

Start at the beginning with a simple clear statement. "I'm calling with some very bad news." Other words might be, "I'm so sorry. This is the nightmare call you hoped would never come."

Anticipate the questions. What would you want to hear if you were on the other end of the line? What happened? Where do things stand now? What will happen next? Often there are more answers than questions. You can say, "I wish I could tell you more. This is all we know right now."

Recognize the limitations of the phone. Most people would prefer to deliver and receive bad news in person. People in pain need to know they are not alone; pain combined with isolation leads to suffering. The most powerful way to communicate the message, "I'm here for you," is with physical presence. Plus, if the person on the other end of the line uses touch as her primary love language, a hug can communicate what words cannot. You can say, "I wish I were there to give you a hug."

Deliver the right amount of information in the kindest way possible. Make it very simple.

Offer to answer any questions—or answer the same question—as many times as they want and need. When people hear bad news, they can only let so much in. On average patients retain about 30 percent of the information doctors tell them. Same in this case.

Assure safety. People who hear shocking news can do and say things they later regret. Find out if you can call someone to be physically present with the recipient of bad news.

Know when it's time to talk and when it's time to listen. Stay on the phone as long as needed, even if there is just silence.

Many pack leaders put their own feelings on hold until the situation stabilizes. You put sadness and grief on hold, but you cannot skip it. The best way to make the unwanted feeling go away is to feel it.

MANAGE YOUR ANGER AND DISAPPOINTMENT

You're in the doctor's waiting room when a man with a flushed face throws down his magazine and stomps to the reception desk. He shouts, "I've been waiting here for a half hour. Do you know who I am? I demand to be seen this instant!" As you watch him wave his arms, you're reminded of a toddler having a temper tantrum. In fact, you're witnessing a middle-aged man having a temper tantrum.

The stresses of caregiving make it easier than ever for tears to flow and tempers to flare. You may have gotten into situations when strong feelings seemed to hijack your body and direct your actions.

I remember with embarrassment my own out-of-control response when the flight that I desperately needed to be on to meet a family commitment was delayed. Susan recalls standing in the ER after her mother was brought in by ambulance with shortness of breath. She demanded they call the mother's cardiologist. She is embarrassed now that she was so hysterical. The doctors in the ER very capably had her mother stabilized in no time.

Emotional regulation is the process of controlling your emotions so that your actions produce the desired outcome. It prevents social faux pas or even legal crimes. Those with well-developed emotional regulation can identify their feelings and act on them in a way that's helpful for them, their loved ones, and others involved in their loved ones' care. The nature of the response is socially acceptable, and the intensity of the response fits the circumstances and meets social obligations.

Emotional regulation is shaped by your temperament and early childhood experience. It's also a skill that can be improved. Emotional regulation occurs in the brain's limbic system—the brain's emotional center—that develops most quickly during the first three years of life. A loving, trusting environment leads to the best development, but early nurturing marred by neglect and abuse can impair emotional regulation for a lifetime. Both adults and children who feel more attached are better able to regulate emotions.

How to manage anger. Some people will go to great lengths to avoid anger—either their own or the anger of others. They see anger as a destructive force. Anger is a normal feeling that tells you that your safety is threatened or that you have an unmet need. It's the expression of anger, rather than the anger itself, that leads to damage.

You need to get the mad out. Unexpressed anger turns into depression. However, you can find a way to let the mad out that won't hurt others.

The many physical and emotional stresses associated with caregiving place everyone at increased risk for anger to get out of control. Here are some tips that will help you be in charge of your anger, rather than letting your anger be in charge of you.

Some days unpleasant behavior, like your teenage daughter's eye rolling, washes off you; other days it sets you off. What makes you more susceptible to angry outbursts?

- Being hungry, tired, or thirsty?
- Out of your normal routine?
- A cluttered, chaotic, or messy environment?
- Overstimulation?
- Uncertainty about the future?
- In the dark?

You might find that a certain set of circumstances is sure to make your hair stand on end. What triggers your anger? Consider keeping a log.

- Not being heard
- Facing rejection
- Not feeling appreciated
- Not achieving the desired outcome
- Being falsely accused
- Not receiving recognition and praise
- Being treated with disrespect
- Being told you're wrong

- Thinking that you are cornered without choices

Many people feel anger somewhere in their bodies. What are some early signs that you're getting angry?

- Teeth clenching
- Muscles aching
- Interrupt others

What happens when you get angry and how do you recover?

- Is your anger expressed as a quick explosion or a slow smolder?
- When you're angry, do you strike out at others or withdraw?

How do you take charge and manage your anger?

- Invest in self-care.
- Create a nurturing environment free from chaos.
- Learn to create a space between the feelings of anger and your reaction.
- Take time to recover in your own way.
- Apologize when needed.
- Be done. Don't hold grudges.
- Forgive.

How to manage disappointment. Disappointment and guilt are cousins. If guilt is a mismatch between the person you want to be and the person you are in that moment, disappointment is a mismatch between the world as you want it to be and the world as it really is. Life's full of disappointment: Your sister told you she would stay with your kids so that you and your partner could finally have a date, and she cancels. The lab work didn't improve as you expected. You cancelled your vacation plans when your brother took a turn for the worse.

Many of the strategies for maintaining hopes and dreams will help you manage disappointment. In reality, disappointment is the loss of a dream. In your role as caregiver, it's a dream about how people should act and how the world should be: Somehow you thought your parents would be there forever. If people eat well and live right, they shouldn't get cancer.

Many of the strategies for managing guilt will also help you manage disappointment. There is one major difference between these two feelings. Guilt is an inside job. You have control over both your idea of the person you want to be and your action. You might feel guilty about missing your son's ball game. You are the one who believes that you should be at the game, and you're the one who made choices about how you spend your time, and getting your father to the doctor appointment took priority over being at your son's game.

Disappointment, on the other hand, involves things outside your control. You may be disappointed if your son's game, that you worked so hard to attend, was cancelled because of bad weather. You have very little control over anyone or anything other than your own thoughts, feelings, and actions.

FOLLOW DOCTORS' ORDERS FOR YOUR LOVED ONES

*Question: How many psychiatrists
does it take to change a light bulb?*

*Answer. Just one. But the bulb's
gotta want to change.*

Adam's elderly mother fell and avoided the feared hip fracture when she broke the fall with her shoulder. The doctor explained the shoulder injury, although painful, would heal on its own. Adam filled the doctor's prescription for pain medication, but his mother left the bottle untouched. When Adam came home from work, he was upset to find his mother in extreme pain. He offered his mother two pills and a glass of water. She pushed his hands away, saying, "I don't take pills."

Many caregivers—who are in the exam room when the doctor lays out their loved ones' treatment plan—work diligently to follow the doctors' orders.

Your loved one—the patient—may not share your dedication. Carrie says, "I think that 'doctor's orders' should be renamed 'doctor's suggestions.' My husband follows about half of them. The doctor says that the daily walk is a critical part of my husband's recovery. It's a fight every single day."

Assuming your loved one is a competent adult, they ultimately decide which doctors' orders they will implement—

or ignore. Carrie continues, "I love my husband so much I would trade places with him in a heartbeat. I wish I could take his daily walk for him. I can't. In fact, I can't take his medicine, exercise for him, or make the best choices at a restaurant. He's in charge of his body."

As the pack leader, you can influence your loved one's choices.

How do you motivate and support health-related changes in others and in yourself? Sometimes the changes are easy to make, like walking down to the fire department for regular blood pressure checks. Sometimes it's a radical lifestyle change like smoking cessation.

I doubt that there's one formula that fits all, or we would all know it and do it! The classic question is whether you pull out the carrot or the stick. I propose a different approach I call the CAB program: compassion, alternatives, and a buddy.

Change can begin with a healthy dose of **compassion.** There's a reason for everything your parent or partner or friend does, even when it's not obvious. Adam could ask his mother with the painful shoulder, "Mom, you've avoided medication your whole life. I'm curious why." Maybe she says, "Pills are dangerous. My aunt was poisoned by her doctor! He killed her" or "Medicine is for sick people. I'm healthy" or "Medicine is just a waste of money." Until you get to the real beliefs that drive choices, all the logical arguments in the world will fall on deaf ears.

You can ask a hopeful ex-smoker, "What do you like about smoking?" Smoking is a hard habit to break because the list of benefits is so long. Smoking is an effective stress management tool. Smokers frequently leave the stressful work environment, socialize, and have something to occupy their hands and their mouth.

That leads to the next element: **alternatives.** Sometimes it means offering an alternative perspective. Adam could say, "Mom, you're right. Medicine can be dangerous, and people still die from medication errors and drug interactions. A very low dose of a single pain medicine is safer than driving to the doctor's office. Could we give it a try just one time when I'm right here at home?" or "Of course you're a healthy person; you're recovering from a shoulder injury. The doctor says that pain gets in the way of healing. The pain medication will get you back to normal quicker" or "With your insurance plan, you only pay $15 for the pain medication. In this case, you pay zero. It's my treat. It may be the best $15 I ever spent!"

Some people need alternative stories they tell themselves and others before change is possible. Change will not happen if the story reads, "I can't stop smoking. I tried many times before and failed" or "I've smoked for so many years the damage is already done." If someone you know has a different story, tell it! Maybe a neighbor stopped smoking at age 70 and he feels great now. Stories lead to transformation.

Some people need a list of alternative ways for getting the same benefits as the habit they're giving up, like smoking. Maybe carrying a squish ball (occupy the hands) and chewing gum (occupy the mouth) or taking up knitting (for men or women!).

Last, successful people have an accountability **buddy.** They make commitments, often put it in writing, and have to stand accountable for their actions. As the pack leader, you may not be the best choice to be an accountability buddy. Maybe someone else in the family will step up or a lifelong friend becomes a fishing partner. The buddies can tell and retell success stories.

I believe that many unhealthy habits such as smoking and drinking medicate loneliness. Maybe that's one reason the buddy system is so important. It's a way of connecting.

Things are different in this stage of life. You and your loved one now have a profoundly meaningful human connection. That opens the possibility for true life changes.

SPEAK UP WITH THE DOCTOR

You take your loved one to a medical specialist who performs a biopsy. The doctor says on Monday the results should be back within a few days. You hope it comes back soon. You're hungry for an answer, and any answer, no matter how bad, is better than uncertainty. It's Friday and no word from the doctor. What do you do?

A. Continue to wait patiently. Maybe the doctor means ten days when he says a few days.

B. Call your loved one's primary care doctor's office and ask if they have the results back yet.

C. Call the specialist's office and say, "We're sitting on pins and needles waiting for the biopsy results. When are they expected back, and how will the news be delivered?"

D. You call the specialist's office and demand to know the biopsy results.

This is the doctor who will treat your loved one if the biopsy comes back with the unwanted bad news. Which is most likely to get the biopsy results the soonest and the doctor's best care should you need it?

Let's look at a slightly different situation. You try a new restaurant and hope the service is fast. You're hungry. You place your order, and twenty minutes pass with no food. Maybe that's normal for this restaurant, you think, and you don't want to make a fuss. Five more minutes go by and you're out of breadsticks. You notice the people around you who placed their orders after you are already served. What do you do?

A. Continue to wait patiently.

B. Try to catch your waiter's eye with your smile.

C. Attract the waiter's attention with a waving hand and say to him when he arrives at your table, "It looks like you're swamped tonight. I was just wondering when to expect our meal. We're starving!"

D. Stand up, glare at the waiter, and say to him when he arrives at your table, "What kind of place is this anyway? That table ordered ten minutes after us and they're halfway through their meal. I want our meal NOW!"

Which is most likely to get your meal delivered without the waiter's saliva mixed in your meal?

Each answer, A, B, C, and D all have a place and a time. In general, for both scenarios, you have the best chance of getting what you want with C—a polite inquiry and a direct request.

We all agree on etiquette standards that help polite restaurant patrons graciously get what they want. Your mother might not have taught you to identify a pickle fork, but she certainly taught you how to behave at the doctor's office. Most Baby Boomers absorbed the childhood lesson stating good patients, like good children, are seen and not heard.

This old familiar medical etiquette is dangerously outdated. Welcome the new rules for medical etiquette. You must speak up. Here's why.

As stated earlier, nearly 100,000 patients die in the hospital each year from preventable medical errors. That's like a jet plane falling from the sky every day. Most of these errors involve medication mistakes and infections spread by the unwashed hands of health care professionals.

FROM THE FILES OF RESOURCEFUL PATIENTS

My hospitalized patient was having a hard time getting the attention of the busy nurses. No one responded to her call light. She was in need of medical attention, and she knew how to get it. She picked up the phone and dialed 911!

Asking doctors and nurses to wash their hands before they touch your loved one could literally mean the difference between life and death. It seems so simple, but it's far from easy. What, exactly, do you say in this situation? When it happened to me as I sat at the bedside of a loved one—and I had been a surgeon for years—still, I sat in stunned silence as the doctor did a procedure with unwashed, ungloved hands. I didn't want to embarrass the doctor who should have known better. Shame on me.

New modern medical manners for nice patients who want to speak up are not clearly defined or uniformly accepted. Soon we will have a code of safe and polite behavior for doctors and patients. In the meantime, when you practice modern medical manners, you run the risk of offending or appearing rude. However, if you had a choice between erring on the side of being rude or on the side of facing a preventable medical complication, which would you prefer?

Here are some tips:

- Approach your doctor in a spirit of collaboration. You're on the same team.

- Remember to say "thank you" to the many members of the medical team.

- Treat your doctor with respect. Angry outbursts or rude comments will not advance your cause as reliably as simple direct requests.

- Treat yourself with respect and ask others to do the same. You may not have gone to medical school, but you can still think through problems once you have the right information.

- Replace assumptions about your doctors' intentions with questions. Don't assume you know, for example, why the doctor did not call you as promised.

- Be willing to talk about your feelings without judgment. "I'm scared" or "I'm embarrassed" goes a long way.

- Know that you and your doctor can respectfully disagree.

- Recognize that medical care is personal for you.

- Recognize that you want to work with a doctor who places the best interests of the patients over self-interests. The doctors you want to work with will not be offended if you get a second medical opinion, because they want the best for you.

- Use common sense.

Emily Post describes good manners as "the continuous practice of kind impulses." What more could we want from ourselves or expect from our doctors as we build the foundation of modern medical manners?

TALKING WITH THE DOCTOR
ABOUT EMBARRASSING MEDICAL TOPICS

Did your mother tell you, "Always leave the house with clean underwear"? Why? "You wouldn't want to be embarrassed at the hospital if you got in a car accident," she might have warned.

Here's the good news. I have treated hundreds of patients who were in car accidents and never once did I hear a doctor or a nurse comment on the condition of the patient's underwear.

However, the embarrassment that your mother was trying to help you avoid is a huge obstacle to workable health solutions.

Doctors cannot solve problems they don't know about. Ben says, "When I took Mom to the doctor, I found out that the doctor wants Mom to take medication for her high blood pressure. Mom didn't tell either of us that she didn't even fill the prescription. Why? She was embarrassed to admit that she could not afford it. She would rather have a stroke than bring up a topic that brought her shame. Once we figured this out, the doctor prescribed generic medication that I pay for."

Let's face it; certain topics are embarrassing to talk about. I call them the 5 P's:

- Peeing
- Pooping

- Paying
- Procreating
- Playing nicely by not embarrassing others

In an ironic twist, those with the greatest chance of having problems with their urinary systems or gastrointestinal tract are the same people who have rigid ideas about what polite people discuss. Gertrude, my 90-year-old patient said, "You youngsters don't understand how much things have changed. When I got breast cancer in 1962, the words *breast* and *cancer* were not uttered in polite company."

There is a natural tendency to avoid embarrassing topics, but this is a risky practice. One of my patients was too embarrassed to tell her doctor about the blood in her stool. By the time she had bloating, the colon cancer that caused the bleeding was advanced. She literally died of embarrassment.

Your loved one may avoid certain topics because they fear you will be embarrassed. Few parents of any age feel comfortable talking with their children about sex. Studies show that many people in their 80s and 90s enjoy regular sexual intimacy, and they may have valid medical questions that they simply do not want to ask. While Viagra has helped men with erectile dysfunction, it's helped all of us—doctors and patients and caregivers—have more open discussions about sexuality.

Embarrassment seems to be catching. Imagine tripping over a curb, which is much more embarrassing in front of others than when you are alone. Your parent or partner may avoid certain topics to avoid embarrassing you or embarrassing the doctor.

You can coach your relatives or friends to speak up with the doctor despite the embarrassment. Here are some encouraging coaching words and tips:

Advise, "Tell the truth: say you're embarrassed." Coach your mother or aunt or sister to say, "This is really hard for me to talk about because it's pretty embarrassing." At this point the doctor will often step in with encouraging words to make it easier.

Help find the words. Joel says, "My father said it hurt 'down there,' but that's all he was willing to say. I had no idea what he was talking about. He could deal with the question, 'Is it in the front side or the back side?' I got out the anatomy coloring book and asked my father to point to the picture that showed where it hurt."

Help find the right person to ask. Your relative may have an easy rapport with the nurse or the physician's assistant at the doctor's office. Suggest starting with this person. Say, "Trish, could you please give the doctor a heads up. I want to know whether Mom really needs those pills for cholesterol. She hates taking them."

Find the right way to ask. You can ask your relative, "Would you like to ask yourself or would you like some help from me?" Also be sensitive to privacy issues. Ask, "Would you like me to step out of the room?"

Remind your relative the doctor is there to help you, not to judge you. Assure the red-faced patient, "The doctor has heard it all before. Your doctor will not think less of you for asking an embarrassing medical question; in fact, your doctor will think more of you for overcoming your fear!"

"You can do that?!"

Here are some handy ideas and requests for the doctor that may not have occurred to you:

- You can see doctors who are not providers on your plan. You may have to pay more out of pocket, but it could be worth it to you.

- Ask about generic drugs, especially if you're dealing with Medicare Part D. They could be much less expensive and do the same thing. Always ask the doctor for drug samples.

- You can ask for longer appointment times. If the scheduler tells you that you can only be seen for fifteen minutes with the symptom you describe, say that you are willing to pay out-of-pocket for the extra ten minutes.

- You can bring a stamped, self-addressed envelope with you to the doctor and ask the receptionist to send you a copy of the clinic notes, labs, and x-rays. The HIPAA law gives you the right to have copies of your medical records.

- You can tell your doctor how you would like your test results delivered: in person or over the phone.

- You can ask when to expect the lab results to return.

FIND THE RIGHT ANSWER FOR *YOU*

> Let's assume for argument's sake
> that I'm right.
>
> ~*Words on a toddler's T-shirt*

Paul was torn. Should he stay or should he go? When his mother scheduled her cataract operation, she told Paul he didn't need to fly out. Her friends would take care of her. Paul was in the middle of a huge project that could mean the difference between success and failure for his business. His mother just called. She changed her mind. She wants him to be with her when she goes to the hospital.

If only there was a crystal ball to see the future and identify the right choice. Unfortunately, there is neither a crystal ball nor a right choice. You make the best choice that you can with the information at hand and take a leap of faith.

Here are some things you may consider as you make the many choices that impact all members of your pack, including yourself:

Assess the situation and identify the wants and needs. Paul is balancing his need to generate an income with his desire to help his mother get the best medical outcome possible and feel supported in the process. Sometimes you'll find important clues by exploring soft questions, like the reason his mother changed her mind about Paul's presence.

Look for all the options. Paul may think that he only has two choices: stay at home to complete the project or leave to be at his mother's bedside. There are many others. Could his mother safely postpone the operation for a month so Paul could complete his project, or could Paul extend the work deadline? Could Paul delegate portions of the project to others or take his work with him? If radiologists in India can read your mother's x-rays and medical records that are transcribed in Indonesia, you can certainly be in touch with your colleagues no matter where you are.

Factor in premonitions and hunches. Let's say that Paul learned his mother "just has a funny feeling" about the operation. If his mother is not known to draw doomsday scenarios, this is very important information. I cannot tell you how or why, but in my own experience with my patients, I find that premonitions have a way of turning out to be true. Further, those who always predict gloom turn out to be right sometimes, just like a broken clock is right twice a day.

There is no right medical choice. Can Paul's mother safely postpone the operation for a month? That seems like a simple enough question, yet the doctor may not be able to give you a definitive answer. Medical choices, like management of your retirement funds, involve risk management. Just as there is no one right investment portfolio, there is no right medical choice.

Many caregiver choices involve your loved one's health. Do you call 911 or take your husband who is having chest pain to the hospital in your car? What do you do when you learn that the nurses caring for your father in late stages of dementia found a groin lump as they bathed him?

In this world of exploding medical technology, it seems as if there should be right answers. If only you could get the right information, you should be able to plug it into the computer and make the correct choice. It just doesn't work that way.

Two of my patients with virtually identical cancers made very different choices about chemotherapy. The young mother of two children took the aggressive chemotherapy in hopes of being around to watch her kids grow up. The other, an 80-year-old woman with a weak heart, decided against chemotherapy. The young mother made a decision based on her desire to optimize the number of days in her life; the older woman made her choice based on the quality of each remaining day. Each made the best choice for her situation.

While there is no right choice, there is a best choice for your family. As the pack leader, you are often the one who helps your loved one make the big, tough medical choices. You may make the choices when your loved ones cannot make them for themselves.

HOW DO YOU MAKE CHOICES
ABOUT HEALTH AND MONEY?

You might imagine that people make important choices about physical and financial health with logic. My experience suggests otherwise. I believe that most people make health choices with emotion that they justify with logic.

In her book *My Stroke of Insight,* neuro-anatomist Dr. Jill Bolte Taylor describes what happened after a blood vessel ruptured in the left side of her brain. She describes how she experienced the world as she lost more and more of her left brain function. She ultimately regressed to an infant-like state. She describes what it's like to experience the world through the right brain. She says that even though she could not understand the words of the people who came to her bedside, she knew who was telling the truth and who had good intentions.

I believe that your right brain makes the choices that are right for you.

Choose your mindset. While you may not be in control of the events in your life, you're always in control of how you respond to them. Here are some choices you may want to consider:

Laugh or cry? Have you ever noticed the stories you tell at holiday meals are about the disasters? Disaster stories, like fine wines, often have to age years before they transform and delight dinner guests. The time your father's colostomy bag broke on the way to the restaurant. The time you were at the restaurant and your child vomited on you, your friend, and the table. The time you were at the restaurant and discovered that you were too busy getting your mother there and you forgot your wallet at home. It can take years for the worst restaurant experience in your whole life to tickle your funny bone. However, you can shorten the incubation period. What would Jay Leno say about your day?

Faith or fear? You decide whether you take on family caregiving in faith that your best effort will be good enough, or in fear that anything less than perfect means failure. Do you have the strength to get through just this one day after the long, sleepless night, or fear that you will let yourself down and let down the people who are important to you?

What's right or what's wrong? You can think about all the things that are going wrong. Your dad still can't walk after his stroke because his right leg is too weak. Or you can think about all the things that can go right and express gratitude. He can use a fork with his right hand now, and his right leg is getting stronger every day.

Can old dogs learn new tricks? Can you learn new skills, like forgiveness, resilience, or conflict resolution? Can you change the nature of your relationship with people you have known all your life? Experience says a resounding YES! Whether you answer yes or no, you are right.

Is your life a blessing or a curse? You never asked to be in this situation; however, here you are in your current reality. Are you being punished? Why do bad things happen to good people? The book with that title may help you decide for yourself. Is caregiving a burden or a blessing? Those who are the happiest understand that events are events; each person has the power to decide if the events are a blessing or a curse. Whatever you decide, you are right.

TRUST YOUR HUNCHES

After a few years as a practicing surgeon, I noticed that patients were not surprised when I delivered bad medical news. They might be sad or scared, but it seemed as if I was confirming something they already knew. I got curious. When patients came to see me for a breast lump or an abnormal mammogram, I used to ask if they thought this was just a little nothing or breast cancer. Almost every patient accurately predicted the news on the pathology report.

After a while, I even started asking people, "How long do you think you will live?" Much to my shock, most people just spit out an answer. In my first phone conversation with my aunt after her cancer diagnosis, I posed this question to her. She told me that she would live long enough to get her deceased daughter's son, whom she was raising, out of the house. That was over six years, and she turned out to be right!

We have been taught to look outside of ourselves for the answers because, supposedly, those answers are best known by the authorities. On the contrary. I invite you to listen to that small still voice. It contains important information that speaks with authority about the best choice for you.

EXPAND THE CAREGIVING CIRCLE

Erin said, "Sometimes I feel like I've been dropped on a high mountain top, and I just can't get enough air. I need more breathing room to take care of parents and kids and a husband and a job. Before the economic downturn, I would just buy myself time with housecleaners and babysitters and home care workers. We can't afford it anymore. I'm afraid that caregiving demands will suffocate me."

You have always known that you cannot take on caregiving alone. Here's something that may be news to you. **While caregiving has its challenges for everybody, it's hard for different people in different ways.** The most successful caregivers are those who spend time doing what's easy for them and join forces with others for the things that are hard.

You have three basic ways of recruiting help: You can hire people to take on specific tasks, you can accept the gifts of help from friends and relatives, or you can barter.

Many caregivers prefer to hire people to fill in the care blanks. They find it challenging to ask for help and receive it. However, increasing numbers of caregivers find themselves with less money to spend. This is at a time when health care costs more and medical resources are becoming more limited.

What if you don't have the option to hire other people? How will you get help with errands, cooking, or child care/ elder care services that may mean the difference between sanity and burnout? This is a time for creative solutions to make the most of every penny and every moment. Here are three options to consider.

BARTER

My friend Suzy and I stumbled on an arrangement that works so well it feels like cheating. Suzy and I are both single parents of only children. Both of us work fulltime outside of the home. Our children, who are the same ages, often click like siblings. Suzy is an imaginative parent who brings out the best in kids. Cooking, which is a chore for her, is recreation for me. Each Sunday Suzy helps the kids cook up some fun as I cook the meal. We eat, then we frequently enjoy some performance the kids cooked up before dessert.

Sometimes Suzy mutters something about imposing on me since I do the cooking. I quickly remind her that the only thing she is imposing is her belief that cooking is burdensome for me. Plus I'm as grateful for the smiles she helps put on the kids' faces as she is for the meal.

Bartering may be the caregiver's new secret weapon. The idea is simple enough. Each person has a unique thumbprint of the activities they enjoy and the activities they don't like. Let's say you like washing the dishes and don't like walking the dog. What happens if you join forces with somebody who likes walking the dog and doesn't like doing the dishes. Both people are spending their time doing things they enjoy and avoiding things that they don't. When you share resources in this way, it works like magic.

Thomas was frustrated because his brother would not contribute to their sister's care. I coached Thomas to say to his brother, "Jeffrey, I know that you have a good heart and you want to do the right thing. Pitching in with Sally's care while she battles cancer is the right thing to do. Let's figure out how to do it in a way that works for you." Jeffrey was a woodworker who loves to turn bowls. These hand-crafted bowls became the bartering chips that Jeffrey exchanged with neighbors and friends for errands.

Consider forming a bartering community. It may include your neighbors, people at church, or even coworkers. Here are some guidelines to support success:

- Know the things that you do effortlessly, and know that it's not easy for everyone. Some people would do anything to avoid the post office or another trip to the pharmacy. Another person enjoys things that you would rather avoid, like weeding your garden.

- Try to be as clear as possible about what you want and what's important to you and your loved one. If someone is going to take your loved one to the doctor and your loved one places a high priority on being at the appointment a half hour early, make sure that request is known.

- Goodness of fit is important. The energetic person who always runs five minutes late would not be a good person to take the clock-watching loved one to the appointment. You don't need to make character judgments about a person's relationship to time; just make good matches.

- Know that you may need to experiment to find the right jobs for the right people. Sometimes magic happens the first time around. Other times it will require trial and error.

- Know that arrangements may need to change as the situation changes.

Once you know what's easy for you and what's hard for you, you can join forces with others in the same way Suzy and I do.

HERE'S WHAT A CAREGIVER SWAP COMMUNITY LISTING MIGHT LOOK LIKE:

I offer you:	In exchange for:
Two trips to the pharmacy	Bathing my dog
Weekly vacuuming	Taking my kids to swim lessons
A home-cooked meal for four	Mowing the lawn
A manicure and pedicure	A neck massage
Two hours of home maintenance	

STRETCH LIMITED HEALTH CARE DOLLARS

Health care is expensive. One of the best ways to lower out-of-pocket spending is to look at the cost of medication. Here are a few tips:

Review the medication list at the next doctor visit and see if all the medication is still needed. On average you can save 20 percent with this simple exercise.

The medication list often grows like the expanding medical file. Things get added but not removed. You often walk away from a doctor appointment with a new prescription in hand, but when was the last time your doctor told you or a loved one to stop taking medication?

Next doctor visit, bring in a list of every medication your loved one takes, both prescription and over-the-counter. Say to your doctor, "I'm watching each penny this year, and I'd like to reduce my mother's medication costs. Could we review her medication list?"

Ask the following questions:

- Why does she take this medication?
- Does she still need it?
- Can you reduce the dosing?
- Do any of the medications fight each other?
- Is there one medication that can do the work of two or three?

- Are there any lifestyle changes that could reduce the need for medication? (Exercise can make a huge difference, even if it's just a ten-minute walk, for example.)

Inquire about lifestyle changes. Can you alter your exercise or diet in a way that would reduce or eliminate medication needs? Your pharmacist is an excellent resource.

Paulette says, "I have to lose over 100 pounds. No one is going to convince me that a ten-minute walk will make a difference." The truth is that a ten-minute walk could be the start of a health transformation. The ten-minute walk could help lose the first few pounds that will lead to more exercise and weight loss. Also know that even a modest weight loss can help you or someone you care for get off some medications. After checking with your doctor, think about going out for a ten-minute walk four times this week. Many of my patients have told me that this is the beginning of true magic in their lives.

Rethink generics. Do your aging parents resist generic medication because they think brand-name drugs work better? In this new economic reality, it may be time to think again.

Your beliefs about the power of your medication influence the response you get from them. The way the mind contributes to the body's response to medication is called the placebo effect. When doctors study new drugs, one group of patients gets the study drug with the active ingredient, and another group gets a sugar pill or placebo. Up to 20 percent of the people taking the sugar pill get the same measurable response as the patients who get the active ingredient. It's the belief in the sugar pill that offers the result.

How does this work? The mind-body connection is an area of active research that may represent the most promising frontiers in medicine. While the placebo effect may sound woo-woo, it most likely works by a similar mechanism that causes your heart to race in response to fear or your face to turn red when you're embarrassed.

The placebo response predicts that if your parents believe that brand-name drugs work better than generics, they will be proven correct. If they believe that generics work as well as brand-name drugs, they, too, will be proven correct.

How do you motivate your parents to take a second look at generics? It's usually not with fact sheets from the FDA that speak to the logical left brain; it's with stories that are the language of the integrative right brain. Ask the pharmacist to tell stories about satisfied customers who use generics. Ask the doctor if other patients who use generics might be willing to talk with your parents about their experience with generics. The left brain that balances the checkbook dollars may allow your parents to see that generics make sense.

RECEIVE GIFTS OF HELP

Some people find it easier to give than to receive. Others find it easier to receive than to give. A life of health is a life of balance. That means being able to both give and receive.

If you are the family caregiver, you most likely give effortlessly. Many caregivers resist the offers of help that come their way. In fact, it can make them downright uncomfortable. Some caregivers cannot even graciously accept a compliment. "Oh, this is an old dress from the back of my closet."

You know what you think about people who take and take without giving. What about people who give and give and refuse to receive? Could this create similar discomfort?

If you find receiving a challenge, here are some things to consider:

- Think about how good you feel when you help others in need. Would you want to deny others that pleasure if they were to help you?

- Do you want your children to learn to graciously receive? The best way to do this is to model the behavior.

- Think about how much better you can serve your loved one and your family if you're able to receive the help of others.

KEEP YOUR OWN
HOPES AND DREAMS ALIVE

I believe in life before death.

~Bumper sticker wisdom

Hope is a critical ingredient in the lives of caregivers. In fact, one of your primary jobs as the family pack leader may be to maintain hope, even when those around gravitate to despair.

Consider a vase filled with flowers from the garden. Hope is like the vase that contains your sweet-smelling colorful dreams. Dreams, like flowers in a garden, change over the season. No matter what season, there is always a dream that can be placed in the vessel of hope.

In most families the loved one—the patient—chooses the dream, and this dream guides the day-to-day choices.

What do you do when you and your loved one and other members of the trusted inner circle hold different dreams? Most caregivers want the loved one's dream to guide the direction of care.

Here's how you can keep hope and dreams alive and let them guide the caregiving effort.

STEP 1: BEGIN WITH THE DREAMS OF YOUR LOVED ONE.

- **Imagine the big dream.** Ask your loved one, "If you had a magic wand, what would you wish for?" It might be something as simple as a good night's sleep or something as profound as the healing of old family wounds. You may see physical evidence of relief when there's a chance to voice longings, wishes, and dreams.

- **Define the odds.** Let your doctor help you come to a clear understanding of the most probable medical outcomes. Defining the most likely course does not mean that you abandon the hope of even a medical miracle. They happen!

- **Craft the working dream.** There is no right and wrong when it comes to dreams; there's the plan that works best for you with the conditions you face. This is not set in stone. The dream can and should be revisited regularly.

STEP 2: CONSIDER YOUR OWN DREAMS FOR YOUR SHARED LIFE WITH YOUR LOVED ONE.

- **State the old dream.** If your parent is the patient, you may have a belief formed in childhood that they would always be there for you. If it's your life partner, you may have dreamed that your partner would always be the strong one supporting you. If it's your child, you have dreams for the child's future success.

- **Mourn the loss of the old dream.** You will be in a stronger position to support your loved one's new dream as you let go of your old dreams. In most cases this works best when you turn to a friend and not your loved one with your sadness about your losses.

- **Create a new dream that supports your loved one's dreams.** The families that work the best are those dedicated to the dreams of their loved ones. You do not need to burden your loved one with your grief or disappointment that he has placed hope in a different place than you would if you were in his shoes. That's when you turn to your trusted friend and say, "I wish Dad would make a different choice. I want him to fight. I'm sad and angry that he's chosen certain death."

- **Remind members of the trusted inner circle that your job is to support your loved one's choice.** This can be liberating for all involved. You are no longer put in the position of trying to decide what you want for your loved one. Your job is to translate your loved one's dreams into day-to-day choices.

- **Stay flexible.** As medical conditions change, it's important that you and your loved one revisit the dream. That's your roadmap. "Mom, I know you were hoping to walk after your stroke, and you're disappointed that has not happened. We can still figure out how you can live in the home you love."

If you're sad, ask yourself, "Is this the loss of a dream, or a hope I can proactively manage?"

Hang onto hope always, and allow the dream to change. No matter how dark the day, there's always hope.

Helpful Resources

BOOKS AND SPEAKERS

B y the time you become a family caregiver, you've been
around the block a time or two. You accumulated wisdom
both through your successes and through your trials. How can
these lessons help you become a better caregiver?

Here are some of my favorite volumes from my bookshelves. These books have been my teachers. While none are
found in the section on caregiving at the bookstore, each book

offers ideas from other areas of interest that can be applied for family caregivers.

I invite you to go back to your bookshelves and find the special books that have spoken to you over the years. They might be business leadership books or books about gardening. What can they teach you about caregiving? Chances are good that they contain the answers to some of your most pressing questions.

It is with great pleasure that I introduce you to some of my friends:

How to Talk So Kids Will Listen
& Listen So Kids Will Talk
by Adele Faber and Elaine Mazlish

> Excellent resource to help you build listening skills and communicate more effectively with people of any age.

When Bad Things Happen to Good People
by Harold S. Kushner

> At some point most caregivers ask, "Why me?" Rabbi Kushner offers an answer that includes the Divine.

The Dance of Anger: A Woman's Guide to Changing the Patterns of Intimate Relationships by Harriet Lerner

> The best book I know about understanding and responding to a near-universally feared emotion—anger.

*The Five Love Languages: How to Express
Heartfelt Commitment to Your Mate*
by Gary Chapman

Dr. Chapman offers his five love languages and shows you
how to recognize and speak them. Even though the book
is written for building the relationship between mates, you
will easily see how you can apply the ideas to people who
are important to you.

The Gift of Fear by Gavin De Becker

While the book outlines a strategy to avoid becoming a
victim of a violent crime, fear is very much a reality for
caregivers. The lessons for listening to the small still voice
are helpful throughout your days.

*Tongue Fu! How to Deflect, Disarm,
and Defuse Any Verbal Conflict* by Sam Horn

Even well-intentioned people offer unkind words in their
efforts to help caregivers. Learn the gracious response that
will make things better and not worse.

My Stroke of Insight: A Brain Scientist's Personal Journey
by Jill Bolte Taylor

A most remarkable story about a brain scientist recovering
from her stroke. This book offers a hopeful message,
especially if you care for someone with a sick brain.

The Childhood Roots of Adult Happiness:
Five Steps to Help Kids Create and Sustain Lifelong Joy
by Edward M. Hallowell, MD

Dr. Hallowell, a child and adult psychiatrist, offers basic ideas that help families get and stay connected. The ideas apply to children and adults of any age.

Learned Optimism: How to Change Your Mind
and Your Life by Martin E.P. Seligman

Dr. Seligman says that, as he trained to be a psychologist, he learned to make miserable people less miserable. Now he helps healthy people lead fuller lives. In this book, Dr. Seligman outlines steps that help readers live with greater optimism and resilience.

The Disease to Please by Harriet Braiker

I found the contents of this book so helpful that I tried to reach the author to thank her. Unfortunately, she died in her early fifties. This book changed my life.

Be the Pack Leader: Use Cesar's Way
to Transform Your Dog ... and Your Life
by Cesar Millan and Melissa Jo Peltier

An excellent how-to manual. Every place you see the word *dog*, substitute aging parents, sick partner, or healthy children, and you have a formula for success. Plus it will help with your dog!

The Wisdom of Menopause: Creating Physical and Emotional Health and Healing During the Change, 2nd edition, by Christiane Northrup

It just doesn't seem fair. Aging parents have this tendency to require their daughter's care just as she enters menopause. This book helps explain why it's such a volatile combination. Dr. Northrup describes menopause as a time in which women give birth to themselves after spending a lifetime caring for people around them. Brain changes that coincide with hormonal changes make women more irritable and less tolerant of people and demands that take them away from this important task. The book may not make the irritability go away, but it certainly helps you understand with more compassion.

Mindset: The New Psychology of Success by Carol Dweck

Dr. Dweck, a Stanford psychologist, describes two mindsets: the growth mindset, in which you invest the effort and celebrate improvement, and the fixed mindset that celebrates innate talent and effortless successes. She shows studies that demonstrate the benefits of the growth mindset and offers strategies for shifting from a fixed to a growth mindset.

The Verbally Abusive Relationship: How to Recognize It and How to Respond by Patricia Evans

> Many people who are treated unkindly by the people who are closest to them think that's just the way the world is. Many of those people are in verbally or emotionally abusive relationships. Evans describes two kinds of power: one that nurtures the spirit and another that kills the spirit. She helps people with wounded spirits heal.

How to Make Someone Fall in Love with You in 90 Minutes or Less by Nicholas Boothman

> When I was a new mother, I was advised to put on a smile before I went into the nursery to tend to my crying child. Boothman's book offers strategies and tips for creating rapid rapport. While the book is intended to help you meet your life partner, the ideas are helpful with people you have known a lifetime.

Senior Days: Insightful Tales and No-Nonsense Help from the Frontlines of Eldercare by Colleen Nicol with Brian Nicol

> A lively mix of entertaining stories and practical advice for caregivers, both family and professional, from a woman who is a senior caregiver.

For auditory learners: If you're an auditory learner, or you love listening to a good speaker, visit the TED Web site. It contains world-class lectures on ideas worth spreading. Many of my favorite authors have presentations on the site: www.TED.com.

WEB SITES

ACCESS CAREGIVER INFORMATION

You can certainly perform a Google search for <<caregiver resources>> and get an exhaustive list. Once I got over 300,000 hits. Here are some of my favorite jewels hidden in the pile.

- **Strength for Caring,** www.StrengthforCaring.com

In the spirit of full disclosure, please know that I am a contributing expert to this Web site. My bias aside, this is an amazing collection of information from a broad spectrum of experts. The online community has been a source of strength for many.

- **Parent Care,** www.Parents-care.com

Looking for local resources in your parents' community? You may spend hours on the phone. When Bill Gillis led the development of Schwab's online trading program, and needed help for his parents, he saw a big problem and came up with a big solution in the form of his company Parent Care. Now you can get a detailed report of community resources, as well as cost-saving tips from the experts, with one mouse click. Although this is a paid membership site, you quickly reap the cost savings that makes subscription a smart investment.

STAY IN TOUCH
WITH BREAKING MEDICAL AND CAREGIVER NEWS

If you're like me, you often turn to online news sources (who has time to read all the newspapers and news magazines?). Here are two ideas for you.

- Set a Google alert for caregiving news at www.Google. com/alerts. This is a service that allows you to get breaking news delivered to you. You can set an alert for specific topics that interest you, such as "aging parents" or "health care costs." You can experiment with the alert keywords so you don't get overwhelmed.

- Go directly to the experts, like journalists do, at www. ExpertClickNewsite.com. How do journalists decide what to write about? They get press releases from the experts. I have worked with my colleague Mitch Davis, founder of Yearbook of the Experts, to open the insider track to press releases previously open only to journalists. On the home page, in the blue box for "experts," you can click on the link to press releases.

NETWORK

The people who have walked in your shoes offer a wealth of wisdom and understanding. Any number of social networking sites will help you connect with others who have a better understanding about what your life challenges really are.

I invite you to join our community at www.TheCaregiver Club.com. We monitor the site to assure that you are safe when you open up. Plus, experts are available to offer different ways to look at issues. You are welcome, no matter what stage of caregiving you're in, or for whom you care.

ABOUT THE AUTHOR

Vicki Rackner, MD, FACS, founder of The Caregiver Club, has been on all sides of the dire diagnosis: as the patient facing a life-threatening medical condition, as the doctor delivering the dreadful diagnosis, and as a family caregiver advocating for sick loved ones. Dr. Rackner is passionate about offering caregivers what they want and need: to know that they are not alone, to remember they have choices, and to hang onto hope that they will make it.

Dr. Rackner is a board-certified surgeon and nationally noted expert in the doctor-patient relationship. She left the operating room to follow her calling, which is helping caregivers and patients and health care professionals partner more effectively with each other.

She received her medical degree from Boston University in 1988 cum laude. She has treated tens of thousands of patients as a general surgeon and has removed more gallbladders and repaired more hernias than she would like to recount. But as a surgeon, she faced families anxiously pacing the hospital waiting rooms while a loved one was undergoing intricate cancer surgery or biopsy. She was the medical team member who brought good news or bad news.

Later in her career, she taught medical students to think like doctors, while she served as a clinical faculty member at the University of Washington School of Medicine. As an expert witness, she has testified in more than 100 malpractice cases.

She's a regular source on CNN.com, has been quoted in *The Wall Street Journal*, *USA Today*, *The Washington Post*, *Reader's Digest*, *Bottom Line Health*, *Woman's Day*, *Real Simple*, and many others. She has been interviewed on over 100 radio shows, including NPR, *Martha Stewart Living*, and *Health Talk*.

"Dr. Vicki," as she has come to be known, co-authored *Chicken Soup for the Soul Healthy Living Series: Heart Disease* and contributed a compelling story to *Chicken Soup for the Soul Healthy Living Series: Breast Cancer*. She wrote *The Personal Health Journal* and *The Biggest Skeleton in Your Doctor's Closet*.

She offers expert advice on the Johnson & Johnson caregiver Web site www.StrengthforCaring.com.

Dr. Vicki's signature tell-it-like-it-is style, coupled with practical tips about exactly what to do and say, have changed the lives of thousands of caregivers. She donates a portion of the proceeds from her speeches and book sales to some of her favorite nonprofit organizations.

She lives in Seattle with her son, Meir, their dog, Elvira, cats, and fish.

About Medical Bridges. Dr. Rackner formed her company Medical Bridges with the intention of offering bridges: the bridges between caregivers and patients. The bridge between the family and the doctor. Most importantly, the bridge between the care patients want and deserve and the care they're getting.

NOW THAT YOU'VE READ THE BOOK — WELCOME TO THE CLUB!

You are invited to join The Caregiver Club

Other caregiver resources help you manage tasks. The Caregiver Club helps you manage *you*. Founded by author, Dr. Vicki Rackner, The Caregiver Club works with people caring for others who want to

- Avoid burnout
- Manage dark feelings like guilt and anger
- Speak up with the doctor and stretch health care dollars

WHAT'S YOUR STORY?

- Maybe it begins with a crisis. Mom fell and broke her hip.

- Maybe it begins with the doctor's call with the bad news you were dreading.

- Maybe it begins when a small yet significant change, like your husband's inability to find his car keys, helps you recognize that there has been a slow and steady decline.

That's when you realize that your life is about to change in a dramatic way. You're about to join the ranks of family caregivers, supporting aging parents or a sick spouse or an ailing friend.

You will have lots of surprises along the way. You hadn't realized how difficult and time consuming this job would be. You hadn't planned for the out-of-pocket expenses. You hadn't expected to feel so alone and overwhelmed.

HOW WILL THE CAREGIVER CLUB HELP YOU?

You will get practical tips and tools that will help you and your aging parents or sick spouse or disabled child get the most from your days and avoid common bumps in the road.

This includes

- Advice about what to say and what to do to assure that your parents or loved ones are getting the best health care possible
- Ideas that will help you lower the cost of caring for your aging parents
- Renewed hope that you will make it through the tough times
- Hope that your efforts offer a legacy of love

For more information, go to www.TheCaregiverClub.com.

MORE HELPFUL RESOURCES FROM DR. VICKI

The best inspiration meets the best information. The Healthy Living series sandwiches vital, life-saving information between inspiring stories of challenge and survival. Inspiration provided by the strongest women and men who looked this life-changing disease in the face with courage and humor.

Chicken Soup for the Soul: Healthy Living Series / Heart Disease

This book offers heart-warming stories from brave heart patients along with information you can use to enhance your heart health. Whether you're managing high blood pressure, cholesterol or recovering from heart attack or stroke, you'll find inspiration and hope with every beat of your heart.

Chicken Soup for the Soul: Healthy Living Series / Breast Cancer

Inspiration provided by the strongest women and men who looked this life-changing disease in the face with courage and humor.

Personal Health Journal

The Personal Health Journal puts you in control. It contains tips and tools to help you direct your health story. Partner with your doctor more effectively. Understand your health story and maintain copies of your medical records. *The Personal Health Journal* is a place to store your medical records and much, much more.

The Biggest Skeleton in Your Doctor's Closet

This is a great little book! Have you ever wondered: What are the biggest mistakes people make when seeing their doctors? What's the biggest mistake patients make when making medical choices? What's the one thing you should never do as a patient? Is the health care system really that bad, or is this just media hype? What should I know about my health story? Dr. Vicki supplies her answers in this booklet.

All books available for purchase online at www.DrVicki.org.

INDEX

ACKNOWLEDGMENTS

I remember the hot summer day I watched the garbage man open the lid of my garbage can and empty its contents into the truck. From yards away I was assaulted by the ripened smell of decaying refuse literally under this man's nose. As he set down the emptied can, I walked toward him and said, "You show up each week, even in the bone-chilling rain and the heat that creates this awful garbage aroma. I cannot imagine what my life would be like if you didn't come to work in the morning. Thank you." I saw his eyes get glassy as he stood taller and walked back to the driver's seat with pride in his step.

There's nothing like looking someone in the eye, and saying, "I see you, and here's why you're important." I love saying thank you. In fact, expressing gratitude is one of my favorite activities in the whole world.

However, I undertake this acknowledgment section with trepidation. Time and space force me to leave many important people unnamed.

The book you hold in your hands would not have come to be without the web of connections with members of my trusted inner circle, acquaintances, and nameless, faceless strangers. The person I am today is like a montage composed of every experience I ever had. Each success and failure, kind comment and mean-spirited barb, moment of joy and moment of sorrow brought me to this moment in time.

Please know that if you ever touched my life in any way, you have contributed to this book. I thank you.

I extend a heartfelt thanks to these people:

My parents, Jerri Gray and David Rackner, who gave me life and did their very best with a spirited child. My brother, Barry, who showed me the power of laughter. My personal hero and grandmother, Nanny Leah, who always found a way of seeing a brighter tomorrow. All of my family members and their stories that sound more like fiction than fact. Ask me about Uncle Big Al.

My son's father, Larry Jablon, and Larry's mother, Norma, both mensches in their own right. Our ability to forge a new kind of family after our divorce allowing us to sit down together for family meals and dance together at Larry's second wedding is a source of pride for all of us.

My patients, readers, and strangers who have trusted me with their stories woven into my writing and speeches.

My colleagues and mentors and friends I met through my membership in the National Speakers Association, thanks to the encouragement of Shawn Conners: Howard Putnam, Richard Weylman, Patricia Fripp, Alan Weiss, Mark LeBlanc, Steve Harrison, Alex Carroll, Henriette Klausser, Max Dixon, Bill Stainton, Linda Keith, Mark Levy, Mitch Davis, Robert Devaney, and Brendon Burchard.

Writers and speakers who have changed my life: Diane Ackerman, Martha Beck, Harry Beckwith, Jill Bolte Taylor, Nicholas Boothman, Wayne Dyer, Debbie Ford, Malcolm Gladwell, Seth Godin, Jerome Groopman, Atul Gwande, Edward Hallowell, Chip and Dan Heath, Harold Kushner, Anne LeMott, Harriet Lerner, Christiane Northrup, Daniel Pink, Michael Roizen and Mehmet Oz, Tim Sanders, and Martin Seligman.

Cheryl Richardson and the participants of Miraval writers retreat. I smile when I recall the moment I first said, at Daena Giardella's instructions, "I am a writer," even though it felt like playing dress-up.

The Mercer Island Fire Department, my State Farm Team, the SHA community, Mark Somers, Barb Burnett, Anna Ormsby and Tim Gorman.

Rachel Remen who taught me about the healing power of stories for both the story-teller and the story-receiver.

My colleagues who have become personal friends. Sam Horn who creates dazzling works of word art, Susan Harrow who taught me to speak so the press will listen, and Dan Janal who helped me hit some professional home runs, as well as share the joy of baseball with our families.

Dave Balch who helps so many families with cancer. May you see many eclipses.

Doreen Parkhurst who taught me to think like a doctor, live without judgment, and just once order every dessert on the menu.

Judith Lipton who attended the birth of my son and showed me by example how short people can stand tall.

Jana Mochkatel who attended the birth and development of my business, and inspires me by telling the truth.

My parenting coach Barbara Swenson and the mommies in my parenting group who help me undertake the hardest job in my whole life—being a conscious parent. Look for Barbara's book about social currency.

Lisa Pelto who guided the design and production of the book. Marianne McCoy and Kristie Ann Carlon and Marilyn Young who spent the day coaxing pictures out of me.

My editor Sandra Wendel who nurtured me and encouraged me and guided me for years.

Suzy Rotunna and her daughter, Mia, who are like the sisters my son and I never had.

My true-blue friend and birthday buddy Jan Aken. How about a celebration at Benny-royal Hall?

Forrest Mozer, who arrived in my life in the form of my physics professor in 1975 and supported me through my many zigs and zags. Forrest's wife, Jackie, who read some chapters from my book while being treated for melanoma. The card she wrote months before her death became my talisman I carry with me in my purse to this day. I like to imagine Jackie sitting at a heavenly table celebrating the book with Aunt Moo Moo and her daughter Julie and Nanny Leah who died on her ninetieth birthday.

Cathy Thorpe whose wisdom and comments shaped every page in the book.

My dear friend Bill Gillis who shows me by example what it means to make footprints in the snow. Thank you for your belief in me. You remind me who I am when I forget.

And finally the two souls who make my house a home. My four-legged companion Elvira who is always at my feet when I write. Most of all, my son, Meir, who inspires me to be my best, keeps me laughing, and encourages me to leave the computer to play catch and have more fun.